An Outline of
WORLD
ARCHITECTURE

To Dad

Just the sort of excellent choice
we would have made for you
had we thought of it.

love from Janine Peter & Graham

Christmas '76

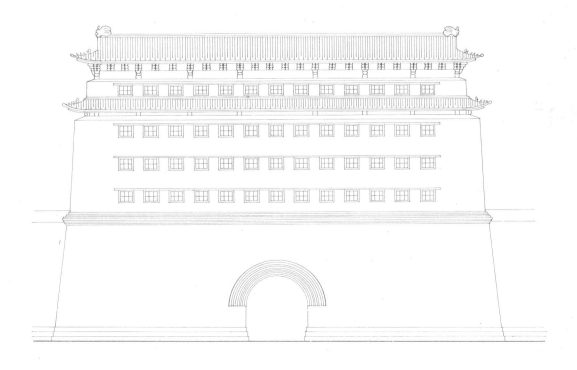

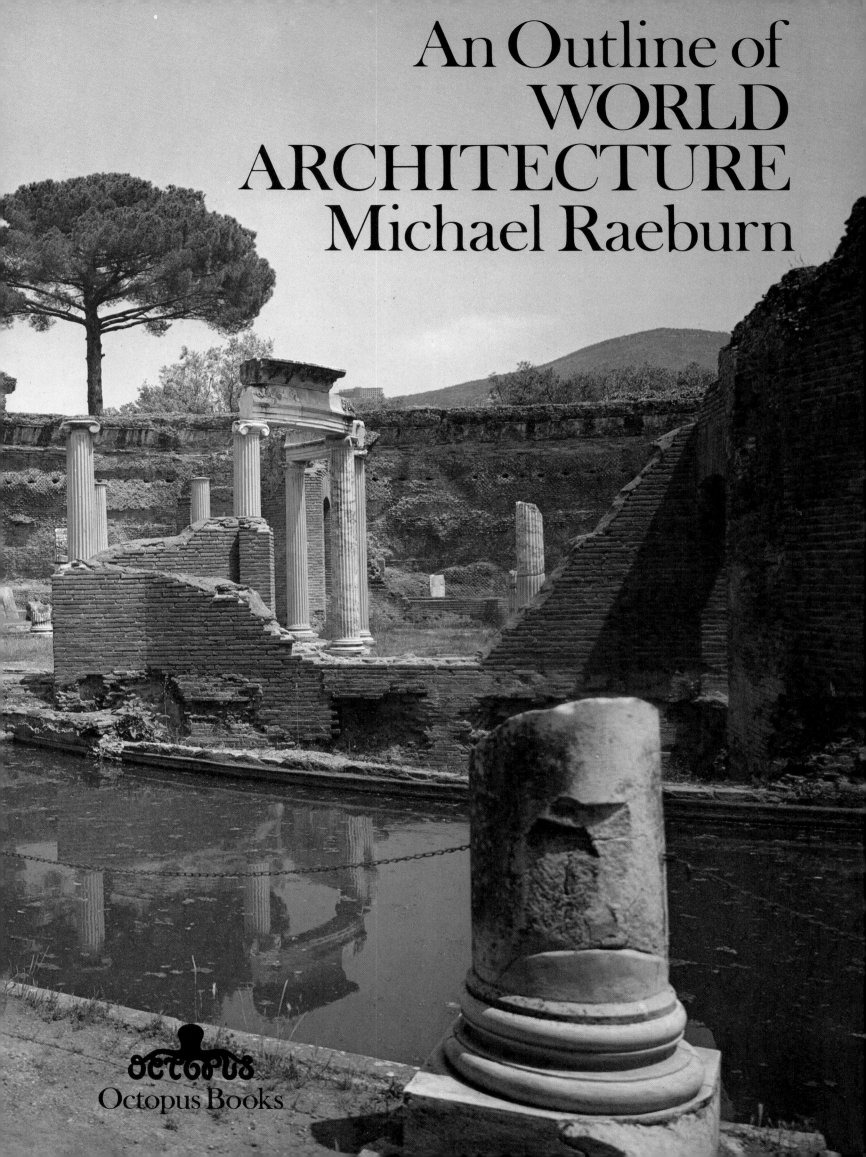

An Outline of
WORLD
ARCHITECTURE
Michael Raeburn

Octopus Books

FOR
ISABELLA
AND
CHRISTINA

First published 1973 by
Octopus Books Limited
59 Grosvenor Street, London W1

ISBN 0 7064 0256 1

© 1973 Octopus Books Limited

Distributed in USA by
Crescent Books
a division of Crown Publishers Inc
419 Park Avenue South
New York, NY 10016

Distributed in Australia by
Rigby Limited
30 North Terrace, Kent Town,
Adelaide, South Australia 5067

Produced by Mandarin Publishers Limited
14 Westlands Road, Quarry Bay, Hong Kong

Printed in Hong Kong

ENDPAPERS **The Classical
Orders according to
Alberti.**
Showing the various
systems of proportions; the
Orders are (*left to right*)
Tuscan Doric, Doric,
Ionic, Corinthian and
Composite.
HALF-TITLE **Outer tower
of Ch'ien Lou gate,
Peking (original form);**
Ming dynasty.
TITLE-PAGE **The round
island villa, Hadrian's
Villa, Tivoli;** AD *118–125.*

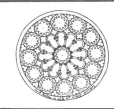

Contents

Introduction

THE MONUMENTAL CIVILIZATIONS

GREECE AND ROME

THE CHRISTIAN MIDDLE AGES

THE ISLAMIC ERA

THE RENAISSANCE

THE CIVILIZATIONS OF THE EAST

REVIVALS

MODERN MOVEMENTS

Introduction

Of all the fine arts architecture is alone in serving utilitarian purposes. Yet, although technical developments have played their part, architectural history is primarily the history of an art form, and the present book aims to show in outline the succession of architectural styles and their relationships to one another. At the same time, there are other factors which condition the way a building is designed and constructed, and attention will be drawn to these too in various examples throughout the book; if we want to know about a work of architecture there are a few simple questions that must be asked:

Who built it? A building is not like a painting, which is painted by an artist, perhaps for a patron, and that is the beginning and end of it. Even when a building is planned by one architect and carried out according to his plans, there will be many other hands at work on it; the big architectural partnerships of the present day will enlist the help of consultant engineers and other specialists both in preparing their plans and in supervising construction work, and in a period when architecture relies heavily on decoration, as in the eighteenth century in Europe, there were sculptors, stuccoists, fresco painters, stained glass painters, as well as the master masons at work, all with their own measure of freedom. The more craftsmen there are who are making an original contribution, and the longer a work is in the building the more the 'architect's' significance recedes into the background. Although the names of many of the artists and craftsmen who were responsible for the great churches of the Middle Ages are known, there are very few cases where one would attribute to one of them the authorship of a building in the sense one talks of a building being by Christopher Wren or Frank Lloyd Wright. They were generally master masons and the status of the architect was only gradually improved in the Renaissance period. Even so, many of the greatest names of that and earlier periods were only architects on the side, or came to architecture indirectly. There were painters (Raphael, Pietro da Cortona), sculptors (Michelangelo, Bernini), mathematicians (Wren and Guarini, as well as the two architects of the sixth-century Santa Sophia in Istanbul), goldsmiths (Brunelleschi), garden designers (William Kent), stage designers (Longhena, Juvarra), military engineers (Hildebrandt, Neumann and the Roman Vitruvius), civil engineers (Thomas Telford), a playwright (Vanbrugh), and many others, while the Renaissance architect Alberti was 'playwright, musician, painter, mathematician, scientist and athlete as well as architect and architectural theorist'.

In addition to the architects, there are the patrons. They have often been of such importance as to be thought of as the real authors of their buildings. One will often read of 'Abbot Suger's church of St Denis', or 'the palace-monastery of the Escorial built by Philip II of Spain'. In cases like these the patron has been responsible for the scheme adopted and the architects have tried to interpret his intentions. In the past the greatest patrons have been kings and emperors, wealthy men, monasteries, churches and religious powers; nowadays the architects work with planning committees and public authorities. When we ask 'who built it?' we want to know a lot more than the name of the architect.

When was it built? Sometimes we will know from the records when a building was planned, how long it took to execute and when it was completed; but often architecture has to be dated from the stylistic features it displays, and frequently it will show evidence of several building campaigns, either in a fairly consistent manner or in a great variety of styles. Sometimes the function of a building is changed and alterations are made; occasionally ruined buildings are used as part of the structure of a new building, or elements from them are incorporated. Sometimes, as in Japan, ancient buildings are reconstructed again and again in their original form. On a broader scale, there is no simple pattern of one style succeeding another. Even if one takes only the western tradition, where the general trend of stylistic development has been common to the whole area, one finds not only great local variation within a style but also that comparable developments have occurred at quite different times in different places and even at quite different times within the same locality. By contrast, in some instances stylistic innovations have been adopted with extraordinary speed in places great distances apart. Within one general tradition the great varieties in style generally show a parallel development, but each at its own erratic pace. This means that the broad divisions of western architecture since the early Middle Ages— Carolingian, Romanesque, Gothic, Renaissance, Mannerist, Baroque, Rococo, etc.—cannot be tied down to any firm dates, and in one place the prevailing style will be elaborate Gothic, in another Renaissance, in another again a transitional mixture of the two.

How was it built? This depends on two main factors, the knowledge of constructional techniques and the availability of materials. At least until the nineteenth century, which introduced the structural use of iron and, later, steel, the basic repertory of building methods was very small. Among primitive peoples and in the early civilizations the local materials were almost always the determining factor, and the styles they evolved had a strong influence on later architecture as their societies became more highly developed. It is impossible within the scope of this book to include a detailed discussion of primitive and domestic architecture, but some examples are illustrated in this introduction to show materials and techniques which have left their mark on more sophisticated styles.

The basic building materials are wood, reeds and thatching, stone of many varieties, and mud, which may also be made into sun-dried brick or, for much

greater strength, kiln-fired brick; concrete and cement are made from crushed stone, sand and rubble bound with lime. Where wood was used, the post and lintel (a horizontal beam supported on two posts) was the normal method of construction, and this was carried over even when other materials came to replace wood. The typical form of a Greek temple reproduces in stone what was originally a wooden structure, and even much of the formal detailing seems to be derived from the wooden model. Mud and mud-brick buildings had massive, thick walls with small openings for doors and windows, and these forms too were carried over into monumental stone architecture. The earliest form of building in stone was probably rock-cut architecture, generally the enlargement of an existing cave to form a planned interior space, often with a monumental entrance carved in the rock as well; this technique was developed until whole buildings, exterior and interior, were carved out of the living rock, as at Lalibela in Ethiopia and in some Indian temples. Later still, stone buildings were erected of rough stone, which was then carved in situ as if it were a natural rock. Stone has in general been the commonest material used for monumental building in high cultures, though not in every case. In Persia and Mesopotamia, where there is a great shortage of building stone, brick construction remained the norm, but from earliest times the brickwork was covered with a facing of stone or of ceramic tiles (or occasionally metal), both for decoration and for greater durability; all the tiled architecture of the Islamic world from Portugal to India has its origins in the mud-brick cities of ancient Mesopotamia. In China and Japan wood remained the normal building material, except for fortifications, and post and lintel construction was elaborated into a complex system of brackets to support the roof.

The Chinese and the Greeks exemplify one attitude towards constructional techniques that runs through the history of architecture; they were not interested in structural innovation, but concentrated on bringing to perfection the methods they had chosen. Both were familiar with the arch, but neither saw any need to introduce it into their monumental buildings; they had satisfactory roofing techniques already. But the arch, and the vault which developed from it, enormously enlarged the scope of architecture; without them the only way to support a roof over a large area was with rows of columns, forming what is known as a hypostyle hall, while large-scale bridges were out of the question. The arch, the vault and the dome (also a logical development from the arch) were all known in the ancient Near East, but it was the Romans who realized their full structural possibilities and applied them to architecture. The Romans are at the opposite pole to the Greeks or the Chinese and the development of Roman architecture is characterized by the increasingly daring application of engineering techniques, partly influenced by their superb bridges and aqueducts. However, in general new structures have been developed to fulfil architectural needs, and architecture is often at its least successful when a deliberate attempt is made to exploit new technology without there being any real necessity to do so. The technical innovations of the Gothic style (see p. 40) are the reverse of this; they came entirely from the architecture itself and, by enabling buildings to be constructed on a skeleton framework, enormously increased architects' flexibility. In the nineteenth and twentieth centuries the developments of metal technology have also been carried forward by architecture and have made possible the construction of high-rise buildings on a steel frame, but the most fundamental step was taken by the builders of the Gothic cathedrals, and the real developments of

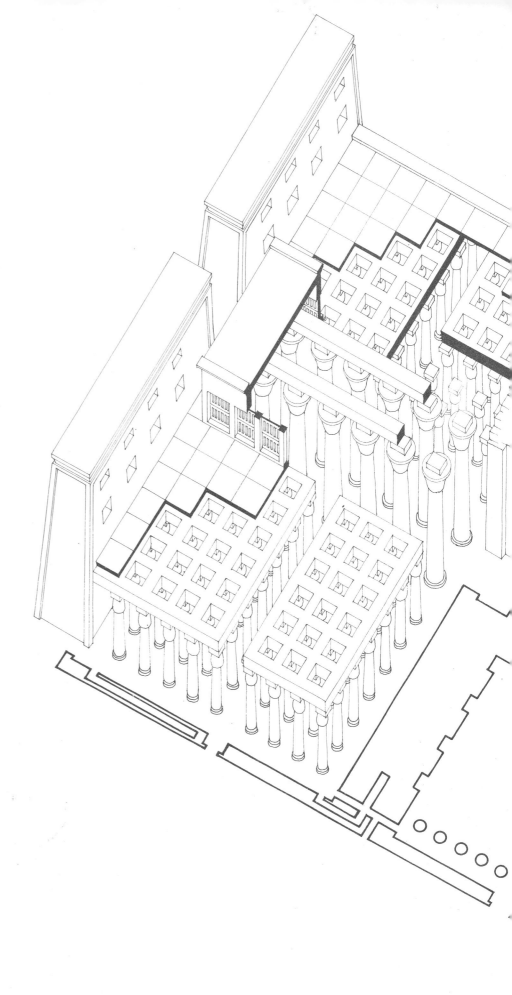

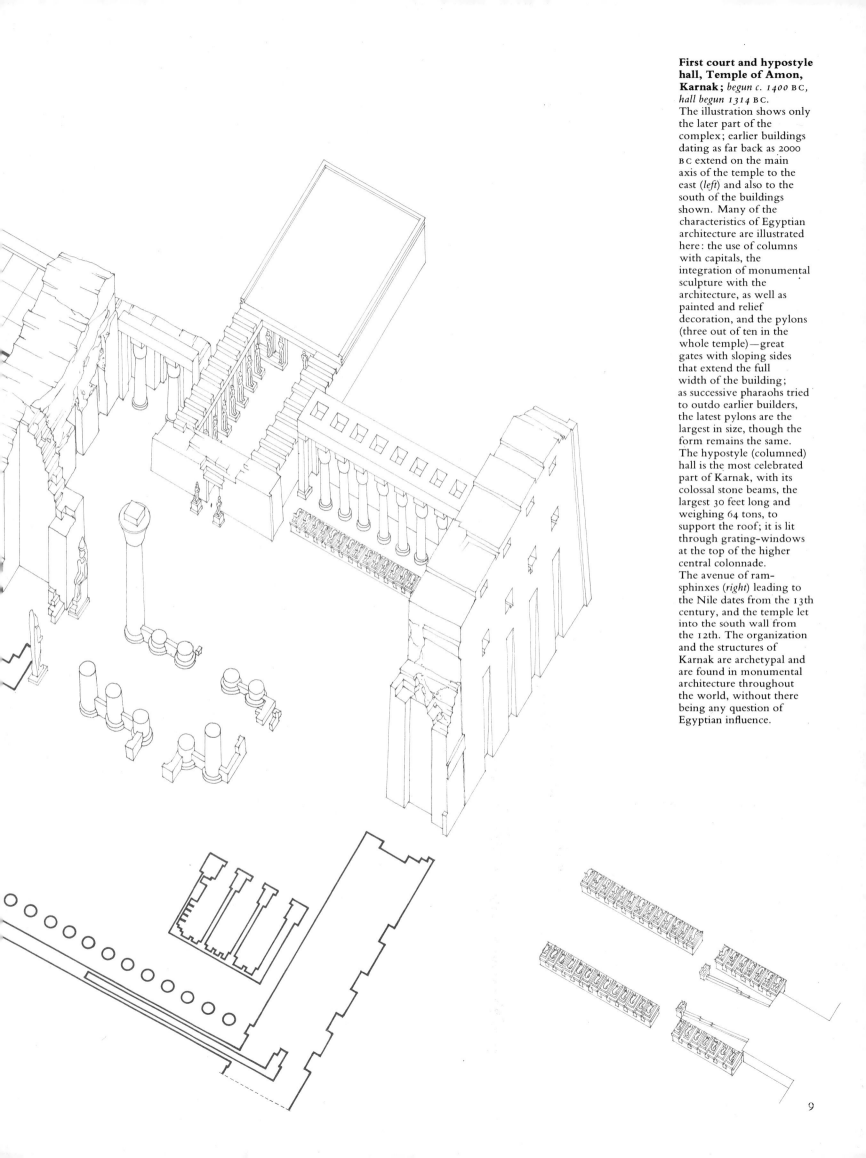

First court and hypostyle hall, Temple of Amon, Karnak; *begun c. 1400 BC, hall begun 1314 BC.*
The illustration shows only the later part of the complex; earlier buildings dating as far back as 2000 BC extend on the main axis of the temple to the east (*left*) and also to the south of the buildings shown. Many of the characteristics of Egyptian architecture are illustrated here: the use of columns with capitals, the integration of monumental sculpture with the architecture, as well as painted and relief decoration, and the pylons (three out of ten in the whole temple)—great gates with sloping sides that extend the full width of the building; as successive pharaohs tried to outdo earlier builders, the latest pylons are the largest in size, though the form remains the same. The hypostyle (columned) hall is the most celebrated part of Karnak, with its colossal stone beams, the largest 30 feet long and weighing 64 tons, to support the roof; it is lit through grating-windows at the top of the higher central colonnade. The avenue of ram-sphinxes (*right*) leading to the Nile dates from the 13th century, and the temple let into the south wall from the 12th. The organization and the structures of Karnak are archetypal and are found in monumental architecture throughout the world, without there being any question of Egyptian influence.

recent times have been primarily in the field of materials
—metals, glass, reinforced and precast concrete.

Why was it built? In the first place, obviously for pro-
tection, against the climate, against wild animals and
against enemies; then, as society becomes differentiated,
buildings take on more specific utilitarian functions,
some as living units for families or other small groups;
others—from the long-houses of the Dayaks in Borneo,
to European monasteries, schools and, now, apartment
blocks—for community living; others, markets and
guild-halls, for commerce; churches, mosques, temples
and theatres for ritual performances; while the last two
hundred years have seen a proliferation of functions
requiring offices, factories, garages, airports, radio
towers, laboratories, sportsdromes, etc.

It is significant that the least obviously utilitarian, the
religious buildings, account for far the largest part of important architecture until very recent times (nearly half
the illustrations in this book are devoted to religious
buildings). The effort and ingenuity devoted to these
buildings should make it clear that, although we should
take it for granted that architecture must fulfil its utilitarian function efficiently, it is not this that necessarily
determines its form or its scope. A building represents
something; it embodies an attitude of the person or
society who built it and displays it for all to see. Under-
standably, the qualities people are most anxious to show
off—to their gods, to fellow-members of their own
society and to rival societies—are their piety and their
power; so their churches and temples, houses and
palaces must be bigger, or more richly decorated, or
more daringly constructed, or of more modern design
than anyone else's. The man who builds a palace greater
than the Emperor's may be laying claim to the Empire,

ABOVE **Screen,
St Etienne-du-Mont,
Paris;** *P. Delorme, c. 1545.*
This illustrates an
architect's response to the
challenge of adding to an
older building: Delorme
(*see* p. 57), to whom the
screen has been firmly
attributed, was the leading
architect in the modern
Renaissance style in France,
while the body of the
church, though begun only
at the end of the 15th
century, was entirely in
the Gothic style.
His solution was to adopt
Renaissance detailing,
while making concessions
to the forms of late Gothic
architecture.
LEFT **Aqueduct at Izmir,
Turkey;** *Roman, restored
by the Byzantines.*
Aqueducts, bridges and
many other works of
engineering (although they
cannot be considered in
detail in the present book)
have often decisively
affected architectural
styles and constructional
methods, and there have
been many important
engineer-architects,
particularly in the Roman
period and in the past two
hundred years.

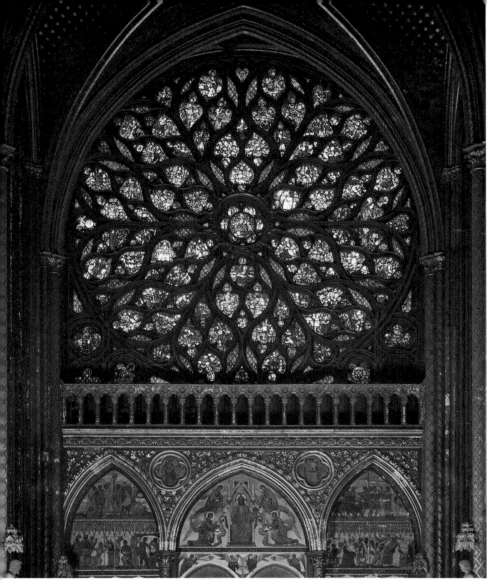

architects we should be aware that this can mean many different things.

So what? A work of architecture is not just a structure built by and for certain people at a particular time and in a characteristic style, using available materials and constructional skills, to fulfil a given utilitarian or symbolic function. It is also a work of art, and the architect and his associates use a great wealth of techniques and devices to achieve effects of beauty and harmony, grandeur and drama. Although they will always be working within a particular style and tradition, the basic aesthetic considerations remain the same, and this is true whether they are assuming a complex style in a selfconscious way (like the Neo-Gothic architects of the nineteenth century), working with awareness within a living tradition, or, like primitive peoples, building completely unselfconsciously.

In the first place, the architect is working with space as well as with solid walls, and the balance between solid and void is his most basic consideration. On the outside he has a choice whether to make the transition from solid to void abrupt or gradual. A solid brick wall leaves absolutely no doubt where the outside space ends and the building begins, but as soon as there is even one window in it the two begin to interpenetrate. There are occasions when architects have wanted to make this transition as abrupt as possible—either to present a hostile exterior, as in a fortified castle, or as a reaction against overelaborate styles, like the early Neo-Classical architects—but more often various means are used to achieve some measure of interpenetration, either by giving less rigid definition to the wall, by extending the building out into the space, or by allowing the space into the building. If a wall is curved, particularly with opposing concave and convex curves, if the surface is broken up with elements set forward or set back or with elaborate decoration, it begins to appear less solid; if there is a colonnade or a loggia in front of it, it becomes impossible to know where the space ends and the building begins, and this ambiguity can be extended if a building is approached by a flight of steps. The use of windows is another method, since they are essentially openings in the wall, breaking down its solidity. The use of whole walls of glass, sometimes on an enormous scale, in some modern buildings is essential, given the starkness of the style; a building like the Commonwealth Promenade apartments in Chicago (*see* p. 120) would be intolerable with solid walls.

Inside the building a similar situation exists, but the architect has much wider opportunities of manipulating interior space. Here, if the confrontation between walls and space is very abrupt, there will be a strong sense of

ABOVE **Rose window, Ste Chapelle, Paris;** *after 1485.* Glass can be made one of the architect's most effective materials. The upper walls of the Ste Chapelle are almost glass screens, and the triumph of void over matter that the Gothic architects sought was heightened by the effect of insubstantiality, of colour and light, that stained glass windows created.

and the town which builds a higher church than its neighbour's is trying to assert its superiority. Apart from this, many buildings have a symbolic function; the Byzantine church is a representation of Heaven on earth, and the layout of a Hindu temple is a symbolic world map. In many societies there is too a very concrete conception of life after death, and the Egyptians were said to have regarded their dwelling-house as a temporary lodging and their tomb as a permanent abode. The many examples of funerary architecture which are among the masterpieces of world architecture, from the Pyramids to the Taj Mahal, also serve to demonstrate the representative and symbolic functions of architecture. When 'functionalism' is laid down as an ideal for

RIGHT **House with cast iron balconies, Melbourne;** *19th century.* The intricate patterns that can be made with iron have been used in architectural decoration since the Middle Ages, though it was not until *c.*1800 that structural use was made of iron in architecture.
FAR RIGHT **Matting tent of the Kurtei tribe, Niger.** Among primitive peoples in tropical climates, where most work is done out of doors, the dwelling need not let in much light, but must provide shelter against extremes of heat. Decorative patterns are woven into the matting.

LEFT **Ghorfas,
Médenine, Tunisia.**
These are dwellings and
granaries of the Berber
peoples, made of masonry
cemented with mud.
The materials used and the
way the buildings are piled
up close together helps to
keep them cool during the
heat of the day and prevents
the sudden drop in night
temperatures being felt.

TOP LEFT **Reed huts of
Uro Indians, Peru.**
Reeds were one of the first
constructional materials in
many parts of the world,
and reed forms often
survive in the decoration
of early stone monuments.
ABOVE **Inca masonry,
Ollantaitambo, Peru.**
Note the projections on
some of the stones, enabling
them to be lifted more easily.

OPPOSITE TOP **Collar-
beam roof of tithe-barn,
Glastonbury;** *c.1330.*
Much of the appeal of the
English timber roofs (*see
also* p.39) lies in the fact
that no structural members
are hidden and that every
one is essential to the
support of the roof.
OPPOSITE **Chapel
of the Holy Shroud,
Turin;** *Guarini, 1667–90.*
In a building of great
sophistication, the same
delight is shown by the
architect in displaying the
structure, to create—in
conjunction with the effect
of light coming from a
hidden source—an
intensely dramatic effect.

enclosedness, claustrophobic or cosy according to the
context, and the techniques of breaking up a wall surface, allowing wall and space to interpenetrate, can be
used to give a feeling of greater openness. This can be
increased still more by paintings in false perspective on
walls or ceilings, or by making a wall out of mirrors.
However, whereas exterior space is undefined, interior
space is made up of volumes defined by the architectural
shell, and these are part of the architect's raw material.
The first requirement is that they should be of satisfying
proportions, and since earliest times architects have relied
on the most basic geometric forms, square, rectangle and
circle, and the simplest arithmetical ratios to achieve
this. The application of geometry can be as straightforward as in the single- and double-cube rooms of Palladio
or Inigo Jones, or as complex as the churches of Borromini (*see* p. 67), which are built up on a structure of
triangles. An overall geometric pattern largely based on
triangles was also fundamental to the design of the great

Gothic cathedrals, even when their building was the
work of many hands over several decades, while the
oval was an important element in many Baroque buildings. In general, the more complicated the geometry the
more the space is opened out, and at times when a sense
of perfect equilibrium between solid and void is the
ideal (as in the early Renaissance) the forms will be very
clearly defined and based almost entirely on the square
and the circle. The proportions will also be related
closely to the human scale. Architecture only takes on
meaning in relation to people, and for the humanist
architects of the Renaissance, who based their theories
on the humanistic ideals of ancient Greece, the basic
units of measurement were related to human proportions. At other times, however, when architecture is
designed to impress or to create a sense of awe, a super-
human scale will deliberately be adopted, and even
though the same system of proportions is followed an
entirely different effect is achieved. Compare the Par-

thenon in Athens with one of the gigantic Hellenistic temples at Baalbek or Palmyra (p. 27), and then again with a miniature temple designed as a garden pavilion, and the importance of scale will be clear.

The same contrast between harmonious equilibrium and more impressive and dramatic architecture can be seen in the use of light. The architect can place the windows to give bright, even lighting to an interior, but he can also have very dim lighting giving a sense of dark mystery, as in many Byzantine churches, or again he can produce concentrations of light from hidden windows to create highly theatrical effects.

Space and light are, finally, products of the volumes and surfaces of the building itself. The architect will normally want a harmonious or impressive arrangement of the masses of his building, and the articulation—dividing-up—of the outside walls can be made to contribute to the required effect. The geometric framework is again a basis and can be emphasized by the use of a formal system like the Classical Orders (see p. 22) or may be implicit in the arrangement and emphasis of windows and other elements. Much can be made of the tension between vertical and horizontal elements, and if an effect of soaring height is wanted the verticals will be stressed, whereas emphasis on horizontals can give a greater sense of weighty monumentality. At the same time the surfaces can be enlivened and given more movement by sculptural decoration, by the play of curves or diagonals, and by the use of contrasting textures and colours. The architect has an inexhaustible variety of materials at his disposal, and he can use the natural textures, or they can be painted or faced.

All these considerations apply also to interior architecture, and it is important that exterior and interior should be closely related, not only in the style of their decoration. A highly dynamic façade will be out of place on a building with a cool, monumental interior, and a strong vertical emphasis outside should be matched by the same verticality inside. Similarly, a façade should reflect the internal arrangement of a building—not for purist reasons, but because otherwise the harmony in the transition from exterior to interior is destroyed. This sense of awkwardness and inappropriateness is often felt when later additions are made to a building by an architect with insufficient skill or sensitivity.

Not only should a building have this inner consistency, it ought also in a broader context to be related to its surroundings. The siting of a building or complex of buildings—in a landscape or a townscape—should be as much a function of the architect as designing the architecture itself, and again he may aim to create a harmonious or a more dramatic impression. He may work on a strictly formal plan with marked symmetry and strong orientation (which often has symbolic as well as aesthetic value), or create a studied—or genuinely unselfconscious—informality; if the building is to be set in a garden (an artificial landscape), that too should reflect the same attitude. The task of the architect requires enormous versatility, and clearly almost every one of the buildings illustrated in this book embodies the work of many hands. I have tried to confine the illustrations to buildings which are still standing, and the drawings are designed to clarify constructional methods, not in any case to be reconstructions. But no photographs are adequate to give a proper impression of works of architecture, nor, luckily—unlike musical recordings and reproductions of paintings—can they make them overfamiliar and so take the edge off the real experience of seeing them for oneself. The aim of this book is to suggest to the reader what he should look for in a building and what facts to find out about it to increase his enjoyment and appreciation of architecture.

CHAPTER I

THE MONUMENTAL CIVILIZATIONS

The first evidence of human civilization can be seen in man's attempt to master his environment, to shape it according to his needs and wants. Nomadic peoples living by hunting and gathering used caves and other natural structures as shelter, but with the beginnings of agriculture and the domestication of animals settled communities developed, and they made the first primitive structures that may be called architecture. Some of these served simply as dwelling-places for a family or community, but others show a further stage of development and were intended not for practical purposes, but as shrines for spirits or gods, or places for ritual performances. The most familiar examples from Europe are the painted caves in south-western France and in Spain and the megalithic structures which are to be found throughout the continent. In either case the monuments are isolated examples of the cultures of the people who built them, about whom we know practically nothing else; but already they exemplify certain architectural characteristics that will constantly recur: the desire for decoration, considerations of symmetry and orientation in artificial constructions, the choice of a site which imposes certain relationships between the monument and its environment.

Older than the megaliths are the early monuments in the Middle East, which are also more extensive than any of the European remains. Around 3000 BC, there were urban civilizations of considerable sophistication in three main areas: in Egypt, in Sumer (Iraq) and in north-west Pakistan in the Indus valley. The excavations of Mohenjo-daro on the Indus have revealed a large city of mud-brick houses, with water supply and drainage, built on a grid system of streets. Although the city may date from as late as the second millennium BC, it suggests the sort of urban development we should imagine around other great monuments that have survived elsewhere. In Sumer there are remains of a number of *ziggurats*, vast stepped temples placed in large precincts, built mostly of mud-brick reinforced with plaited reeds, bitumen and kiln-baked brick, but sometimes using stone and also metal for facing and for decoration.

The pyramids, the most typical buildings of the Egyptian Old Kingdom, are gigantic funerary monuments, artificial mounds over the graves of the pharaohs, but they too formed part of a larger architectural complex, a necropolis, or city of the dead. The most familiar pyramids are the three at Gizeh, of which the greatest, that of the pharaoh Cheops, was for nearly five thousand years the highest building in the world; but the earliest pyramid (*c.* 2780 BC), stepped like the temples of Sumer, was built by King Zoser in his necropolis at Sakkara. The architect is even known by name, Imhotep, and he planned not only the pyramid but the 'white wall', thirty-two feet high, round the vast rectangular enclosure, the funerary temple and other buildings. All are of stone and are constructed with an astonishing precision,

OPPOSITE **Stonehenge;** *first half 2nd millennium* BC. Stonehenge is the most famous of all the megalithic monuments of Europe, some of which date back as far as 4000 BC and which are found through much of Atlantic Europe and also in Malta. They have in common that they are made of huge blocks of stone (traces of similar wooden monuments have also been found), sometimes, as here, transported over considerable distances, and that they are arranged with a strongly defined orientation. There is no doubt they served a ritual purpose, and they are the most primitive examples of monumental architecture among the Stone Age and Bronze Age peoples of western Europe.

considering that only a century before no large stone
building had existed anywhere. They even contain the
first stone columns with capitals, not yet standing free
from the wall, but to become one of the most significant
elements in the whole future of architecture. The pyramids dominate their landscape and were, and remain,
powerful symbols of the immortality of the divine
kings.

By the year 2000 the political centre of Egypt had
moved up the Nile to Thebes, and here in the Valley of
the Kings vast temples were built, which show many of
the characteristic structures of the great period of Egyptian architecture. At Karnak, the hypostyle hall, supported by a forest of columns, was added to the Temple
of Amon in the last decades of the fourteenth century
BC, and the courtyard in front of it four hundred years
later (*see* pp. 8–9). This temple illustrates how, throughout the history of architecture, a complex has grown
and developed over many centuries, with destruction

and rebuilding of many parts, and yet remains a unity.
The final (unfinished) form of the Temple of Amon
shows an arrangement to be encountered again and
again: the precinct which defines the space occupied by
the temple; the open court forming part of the precinct
contrasting with the crowded enclosed hall; the use of
side arcades to provide transitional areas where the
boundary wall and the space of the court interpenetrate;
and the sense of progression in passing from the first entrance through to the most distant temple buildings, all
aligned on the same central axis.

The second millennium BC saw the growth of monumental civilizations elsewhere in the Mediterranean area,
of which the most interesting survival is the Minoan
culture of Crete. Our knowledge of this centres largely
round the excavations at Phaestos and of the 'Palace of
Minos' at Knossos, which contains many rooms, halls
and corridors. It has been extensively reconstructed—
rather crudely—but this does allow the visitor to gain an

LEFT **Pyramid of King Zoser, Sakkara;** *c.2780* BC. The funerary complex, built by Zoser's court architect Imhotep, of which the pyramid is the focal point, is the first great stone monument. It is on a gigantic scale, the precinct measuring about 610 yards (1000 Egyptian ells) by 306, and the pyramid rising to a height of 195 feet. Inside, shafts, some of them over 100 feet deep, lead to the royal burial chambers, which are faced with granite or in some cases with faience.

BELOW **The Great Pyramids, Gizeh;** *c.2600* BC.
The largest, the pyramid of Cheops, built to a height of 475 feet, dwarfs Zoser's pyramid, yet exhibits an extraordinary accuracy of calculation and measurement—in itself and in its alignment with the neighbouring pyramids. It is faced with polished limestone and is a masterpiece of stone working.

OPPOSITE TOP
Throne room, Knossos;
late 15th century BC.
The restored frescoes of Knossos (based on fragmentary originals now in the museum there) give a clue to the splendour of the palace architecture of the ancient Mediterranean; the throne room is at the heart of the palace, off the main interior courtyard.

OPPOSITE BELOW **Detail of staircase, Persepolis;**
founded c.520 BC.
The buildings of Darius's palace are organized within a rigid grid on a raised platform, with a strongly emphasized axis; at their centre is the throne room, or Hall of a Hundred Columns. The great stair leads up to the entrance gate of the palace.

impression of the massive columns, tapering towards the base, and the vivid painted decoration on both columns and walls. In mainland Greece, the most extensive remains are the royal palace and tombs at Mycenae dating from the fourteenth and thirteenth centuries BC.

The ensuing centuries saw the flowering of a variety of cultures in the area of the Mediterranean and the Middle East, besides the dawning of the era of Classical Antiquity. In Mesopotamia the Assyrians in the north and Sumerians and Babylonians in the south had made great advances in constructional techniques, using the arch, the dome and the vault. The ruins of the Assyrian royal palace of Khorsabad show a huge complex of halls, temples and courtyards, dominated by the great citadel and remarkable for its monumental sculptural decoration, while there was fine relief sculpture in brickwork and brightly coloured glazed tiles in the later palace at Babylon. But much of the best architectural decoration from both cities is now in museums, and a more impressive site is the palace of Darius at Persepolis, with its magnificent relief carvings, which dates from the period of the Persian wars against Greece. We know from Greek writers of the splendour of the Persian court

and the sophisticated administration of their great empire, but Persepolis was destroyed by Alexander the Great, in retaliation for the Persians' destruction a hundred and fifty years before of the Acropolis at Athens, and thereafter Greek architecture dominated the Middle East, while many of the Persian craftsmen dispersed further east and left their mark on Indian architecture.

Egypt alone preserved her ancient culture to a greater extent, and even in the last hundred and fifty years BC Egyptian temples retained traditional pylons and columns with lotus and palm capitals, though they cannot compare with the monumental masterpieces of the pharaonic period. Further to the south, in the Sudan, an important Nubian culture had developed round the city of Meroe, and Meroitic pharaohs had for a time controlled the whole of Egypt. It was a flourishing civilization for many centuries, relying on its sophisticated iron-working and its trading links within the continent of Africa, with Europe and even as far afield as China. Their culture was eclectic, adapting and incorporating elements from many other places, and their temples at Musawarat-as-Safra and Naga show a much less purely Egyptian style than the buildings in the north.

LEFT **Detail of columns, Temple of Horus, Edfu;**
begun 237 BC.
The form of the capitals, based on palm-frond and flower-bud motifs, and the method of construction, using stone beams to support the roof, show how closely tied Egyptian architecture remained to the original buildings of wood and reeds, although they now had a 2,500-year-old tradition of building in stone, of which Edfu shows the final flowering.

ABOVE **Doorway of temple at Naga, Sudan;**
1st century BC.
The remarkable sandstone temples of Nubia show a mixture of styles characteristic of that civilization; the doorway with sloping sides is based on the Egyptian pylon and is surmounted by vulture-winged Egyptian emblems of the sun, the little arches are derived from Roman architecture, while other decorative elements are of African origin.

RIGHT **Western enclosure, Zimbabwe;**
c. AD 1000–1500.
A monument that is modest in proportion to the pyramids, but gives evidence, though tantalizingly incomplete as yet, of an important settled culture in southern Africa.

BELOW **Temple of Tlahuizcalpantecuhtli (the planet Venus), Tula, Mexico;** *c. AD 1000.*
This pyramid, approached by the staircase 30 feet in width, is the greatest monument of the Toltecs of central Mexico; originally it had carved stone facing attached to its sides and the temple itself stood at the top. The basalt warrior figures were then part of the vestibule and colonnade, seen here in the foreground.

In southern Africa, the development of civilization was much slower, and there are few examples of monumental building before the Islamic invasions. A notable exception is the great Iron Age complex at Zimbabwe, in Rhodesia, built and inhabited between AD 1000 and 1500 by a people indigenous to south-central Africa. The ruins are in the form of large enclosures, each of which contained a number of huts, with high stone walls topped by monoliths. The stonework was originally faced with a clay and gravel cement which also served as a paving material. Zimbabwe remains an isolated phenomenon and little is known of the exact function of the buildings or of the life of the people who constructed them, but it provides an example of the widespread incidence of monumental architecture in early civilizations. This is seen even more strikingly in the great temples of pre-Columbian America, which, though of a quite different date, are manifestations of civilizations in many ways equivalent to those of ancient Egypt and the Middle East, both in the sophistication of such things as their calendars and astronomy and in the lack of technological development in so many other areas that gave supremacy to the Chinese or the Greco-Roman cultures.

The main centres are in Mexico, where there are archaeological remains dating to 1500 BC, and in Peru, where they go back a thousand years further. The earliest examples of monumental architecture are the pyramids at Teotihuacán in the valley of Mexico, built of mud-brick faced with stone, mainly in the first century AD. Teotihuacán was destroyed about AD 600, but its influence can be seen in the monuments of the Mayas, who developed a high degree of culture on the Yucatán peninsula, as notable for its palaces as for its temples, and in the Toltec buildings in central Mexico, pyramids to serve the cults of human sacrifice practised by this warlike people. Like the monuments of Egypt and Sumer, these were built to dominate the landscape, and they are decorated with the most elaborate carvings.

The last of the pre-Columbian monumental cultures was that of the Incas, whose empire was built up only in the fifteenth century AD. Their building was characterized by its megalithic masonry, not unlike that of Zimbabwe. It is seen well in the ceremonial buildings of the mountain city of Machu Picchu, the last fortress to resist Pizarro's conquistadors, heirs themselves to two thousand years of high civilization in western Europe.

CHAPTER 2

GREECE AND ROME

The debt of the whole of western civilization to Classical Greece is shown in nothing so clearly as in the history of architecture. The basic elements of Greek architecture—as well as Greek theories of proportion—have been adopted by a continuous tradition of over 2500 years, and are fundamental to all western styles—even Gothic—until this century. In spite of the wealth of material, our knowledge is still incomplete (no full texts on architectural theory have survived, and material prior to the Classical age is very fragmentary), but there are two things which are immediately striking: the fineness of perfection to which they brought their buildings, and their extreme conservatism in the matter of form, structure, even detail.

The earliest temples can be traced back to the eighth century BC, following the dark age of Greece after the destruction of the Mycenean civilization in the twelfth century, yet there is little that survives before the sixth century, since the materials used previously were mainly masonry combined with sun-dried brick and wood. But even the earliest examples show the familiar temple form: a rectangular sanctuary with an open ante-room, the whole surrounded by an outer colonnade constructed on a stepped base; slabs of stone rest on the capitals of the columns to form a continuous entablature, divided into formally decorated sections, running round the whole building; at each narrow end a low triangular pediment, also decorated, often with elaborate sculptures, dictated the slope of the roof, which was of tiles laid over a timber framework. Much of the detail, particularly on the upper levels, was painted. (Although the Greeks were familiar with the arch—from Egypt and from its use in town-gates in provincial Greece—it never had a place in their monumental architecture.)

Not only did the structure become standard at a very early date, but the detailing was just as rigidly determined within one of three systems, known as the Orders, of which the Doric and Ionic are earlier, the Corinthian exceptional until the Roman period, when it became the norm. Each Order varied, not only in the shape of the capitals, which are their most easily recognizable feature, but in the proportions of the columns (height to thickness, etc.) and of the various parts of their bases and entablatures. A standard for each of the Greek Orders (and additional later ones) worked out by the Renaissance architect Alberti is shown on the endpapers. That Greek buildings conform, within narrow limits, fairly closely to these norms is the more remarkable when one remembers that ancient Greece was composed of separate city states on the mainland, whose individual colonies made up an empire that extended throughout the Aegean islands, to Asia Minor (Ionia) and westwards to Sicily and southern Italy.

The main temples in any city were usually contained in a fortified citadel (*acropolis*), though in the Panhellenic

OPPOSITE **Delphi.** The view is taken over the theatre towards the ruins of the 4th-century Temple of Apollo and, on the right, the Treasury of the Athenians (*c.*489 BC). The Temple of Apollo, built on a narrow site on an artificial platform, was one of the most sacred places in all Greece, and the oracle was consulted by men from every city; the surviving ruins are of the sixth temple on the site, which was modelled closely on the previous 6th-century building.

RIGHT **Parthenon, Athens**; *Ictinos and Phidias, 447–432* BC. The most harmoniously proportioned and best preserved of Greek Doric temples, the Parthenon represents the perfection of a tradition of building in stone in forms that are derived from wooden models. It has remained a symbol of the greatness of 5th-century Athens.

BELOW **Columns of the 'Basilica', Paestum**; *mid-6th century* BC. This early Doric temple shows the curved tapering of the columns and the flattened capital in a more pronounced way than the later temple of 'Poseidon' (early or mid-5th century) seen in the background.

BELOW RIGHT **Interior of Temple of Apollo, Bassae**; *attributed to Ictinos, c.420* BC. Although the main colonnade of the temple is Doric, the interior columns, emerging from the wall of the sanctuary, are Ionic; the scroll capitals are no longer to be seen, but compare the graceful bases of the columns with the uncompromising Doric rising straight from the pavement of the temple.

centres like Delphi or Olympia the sacred buildings would cover a wider area. In Delphi, seat of the oracle of Apollo, there are temples and treasuries (smaller shrines erected by the different cities in their local styles) built over three centuries on a magnificent hillside site overlooked by Mount Parnassus. Many follow the main 'Sacred Way', but there is no overall plan—although there were already Greek towns built on the geometrical grid pattern which became characteristic of Roman town planning. In general, the buildings of Classical Greece are sited magnificently in a way that harmonizes with the dramatic landscape.

The most impressive of the early sites is Paestum, on the Italian coast, south of Naples, with three Doric temples, two of the sixth and one of the fifth century BC. It must have been possible in the earlier period for architects to work with greater originality, since both the sixth-century buildings show marked departures from the norm; the massive columns taper to the flattened capitals with a distinctive curve, and in the 'Temple of Ceres' the roof was raised much higher than was usual; but they show the monumental strength of the Doric Order. A more sophisticated Doric is seen in the most famous of all Greek buildings, the Parthenon on the Acropolis at Athens. The architect, Ictinos, incorporated a whole range of refinements to compensate for certain optical tricks (though some have practical value): if all the verticals and horizontals were absolutely straight, the eye would see slight curving or tilting; if the corner columns were of the same thickness as the others, they would appear to be thinner; so the corner columns are thickened, straight lines curved slightly, verticals tilt. The curving can be seen both on the base of the temple, which droops away to each of its corners, and on the columns, which diminish towards the top in a very slight curve. These refinements are seen at their most subtle in the Parthenon, but some can be found in the majority of important Greek buildings, at least from the fifth century. With all this, the Parthenon is a building of outstanding beauty with the most harmonious proportions, and as such a magnificent justification of the Greeks' obsession with perfection rather than originality.

The Ionic Order, characterized by slimmer columns with scroll capitals, was the style of Asia Minor (Ionia) and almost all the most important early examples were in Ionian cities or in their Treasuries at Delphi. In fifth-century Athens it was used in conjunction with Doric, most notably in the porch (*Propylaia*) of the Acropolis, built in five years at the time of the outbreak of the disastrous war between Athens and Sparta. Probably contemporary with this is the temple at Bassae (Vassé) in Arcadia, traditionally said to have been designed by Ictinos. The main colonnade at Bassae is of free-standing Doric columns, but the interior of the sanctuary has ten engaged Ionic columns and one free-standing column, which had probably the first-ever Corinthian capital, made up of a cluster of acanthus leaves. The historical curiosity of Bassae is less striking than its great beauty, sited on a high hill, visible for miles around, and, it is said, so orientated that the first ray of the rising sun would strike the great golden statue of Apollo that was originally there. It is typical of the Greek sensitivity to the relationship of buildings to their environment.

This same feature can be seen in the Greek theatres, of which the main characteristic was the semicircular ramped seating, cut from a hillside and faced with stone. This encircled the area where the actors performed which was backed by a permanent architectural 'scene'. There is a fine fourth-century theatre at Athens, but the best preserved is at Epidaurus.

One of the last great buildings on the Acropolis at Athens was the Erechtheum, a temple which shows the most exquisite workmanship of any ancient building that survives. Its most notable feature is the replacement of some of the columns with female figures, known as caryatids, one of the variations possible within the Ionic Order. It was completed in the final decade of the fifth century, one of the last testimonies to Athenian greatness.

In the fourth century, the greatest monuments were built in Asiatic Greece, but of the Temple of Artemis at Ephesus and the Mausoleum at Halicarnassus, both included among the 'Seven Wonders of the World', little survives, and the succeeding centuries saw the decline of Greece and the rise of Rome, though in Asia Minor Hellenistic architecture was a living tradition throughout the Roman period.

BELOW **Erechtheum, Athens;** *c.421–406* BC. The form of this temple is unusual, since it was built on very uneven ground and had to unite several shrines. It is in a highly refined version of Ionic, using marble and black limestone.

BOTTOM **Theatre, Epidaurus;** *Polycleitos the younger, second half 4th century* BC. The Greeks paid great attention to the acoustical as well as formal aspects of their theatre design.

ABOVE **The Roman Forum.**
Prominent among the buildings to be seen here, looking from one of the surviving columns of the Temple of Castor and Pollux, are in the centre the Spring of Juturna, in the middle distance on the left the circular Temple of Vesta (which was a powerful inspiration to Renaissance architects), and on the skyline above it the huge vaults of the Basilica of Maxentius.

RIGHT **Intersection of main streets, Pompeii;** *1st century* BC.
The picture shows clearly the raised sidewalk and the large stepping stones, by which pedestrians could avoid the garbage and the water that flowed in the street. To the right is one of the fountains that were often to be found at crossroads.

Rome itself offers the first real example of urban architecture, and the whole area of the Roman Forum shows a group of temples and public buildings dating from several centuries, designed both to preserve ancient paths (just as many modern city centres are still criss-crossed by a maze of medieval streets) and to provide dramatic and impressive vistas. Outside the centre there were apartment blocks, and there is no doubt that Rome, as a great metropolis, suffered from many of the problems that are so acute in cities nowadays. Pompeii and Herculaneum, miraculously preserved under the ash and lava of Vesuvius, were smaller and less crowded, and their streets of houses give a good picture of urban architecture in the last century BC, based largely on a network of straight streets running east–west and north–south, though there are some variations.

The greatest monumental architecture of Rome dates from the first century and a half of our era, the years of the greatest power of the Roman Empire. The Romans were far more adventurous than the Greeks and, although they worked within the system of the Greek Orders, these were used with much more freedom, far greater emphasis being given to the development of constructional techniques. Roman achievements in engineering are quite remarkable. They fully exploited the constructional possibilities of the arch, which is

ABOVE **Pantheon, Rome;**
c.AD 118–128.
The dome, which occupies
half the height of the
building, has a diameter
of 142 feet, greater than
that of St Peter's.
It was made of concrete
with the material graded so
as to make the mixture
increasingly light the
nearer it was to the top.
TOP RIGHT **Colonnade
of Temple of Baal,
Palmyra;** *dedicated AD 32.*
This colossal temple has
many unusual features
derived from old semitic
tradition, being set in a
walled precinct and entered
on its long side. The
missing Corinthian capitals
on the columns were
originally of bronze.
RIGHT **Khazna Temple,
Petra;** *c.AD 120 (or earlier).*
The façade is outstanding
both for its finely carved
detail and for the rose-
coloured stone.

able to span greater distances and with far greater
strength than the lintel on two columns; they used concrete as a building material, allowing greater flexibility
of construction, particularly of roofing vaults; and
they developed the dome, to roof a circular area. At the
same time it has to be admitted that the harmony and
refinement of Greek architecture and its intimate
human scale were lost, and the vast monuments of the
Roman Empire impress rather by their size and their
miraculous construction.

With the growth of the Empire, Roman cities were
built throughout the Mediterranean lands and further
north, and much of the provincial architecture shows
imaginative variation on the metropolitan styles. One
of the most extraordinary examples is the façade of the
Khazna at Petra in Jordan, the rock-cut entrance to a
cave temple. Elsewhere in the Near East, notably at
Baalbek in Lebanon and Palmyra in Syria, there are a
number of temples which depart radically from the
Greek tradition, incorporating arches, giant columns
and strongly dramatic effects, which closely resemble
the use made of the Classical Orders by Baroque architects in the seventeenth century. The Roman cities of
north Africa, while less extravagant, have some of the
most beautiful and simple examples of Roman Imperial
architecture.

27

In the later Empire hugeness seems to have become an end in itself, and just as the pharaohs had always wanted to outdo their predecessors by building a little larger, so too the Roman Emperors offered exaggerated symbols of their power in their palaces and public buildings. Two of the most extensive palaces were built around the year 300, for the retirement of the joint Emperors Diocletian and Maximian, at Split in Dalmatia and at Piazza Armerina in Sicily. Diocletian's palace at Split is one of the best preserved and most elaborate architectural complexes of the whole Roman period, but a fortified camp or city rather than a 'palace'. The villa at Piazza Armerina is a much looser grouping of sumptuous buildings, which are based on the villa, or country palace, built by the Emperor Hadrian at Tivoli, near Rome, nearly two hundred years before.

Several of the Emperors had built huge public baths in Rome, the main halls of which exhibited some of the most adventurous examples of vaulting, particularly the Baths of Diocletian, later converted into a church by Michelangelo. But again this was outdone by the last and the largest of all the great halls, the Basilica of Maxentius, completed by Constantine. This had a nave vault and two aisles, each closed by an apse, and the span of the nave was over eighty feet. Basilicas were used both as law courts and as public meeting places, and their form was much imitated for churches on the introduction of Christianity by Constantine after his defeat of Maxentius in 312. Other forms of Roman religious and secular architecture were also pressed into the service of Christianity, many pagan monuments being converted for use as churches. In particular, the small circular building, a form used in Rome typically for a mausoleum, was adapted to the church and to the baptistery; the church of S. Costanza with its inner colonnade supporting a dome is still entirely in the tradition of Roman architecture.

The establishment of Christianity and the division of the Empire after Constantine's death provide real turning points in architectural development. After the secular culture of Imperial Rome, for more than a thousand years, until the secular culture of the Renaissance, the chief energies of architects were devoted to religious buildings, of the Orthodox church in the Byzantine Empire and eastern Europe, of the Roman church in the west, while in the Asiatic and African territories of the Roman Empire, Christianity was soon to yield to the new forces of Islam.

ABOVE **Porta Nigra, Trier**; *early 4th century* AD. Trier was the northern capital of the late Roman Empire, and the architecture of this gate (which is unfinished) was a forceful declaration of Roman imperial power.
TOP LEFT **Colonnaded streets and arch of Trajan, Timgad, Algeria**; *2nd century* AD. Timgad was founded by the Emperor Trajan as a settlement for veterans in AD 100; it was constructed according to a strict grid pattern and offers one of the clearest examples of developed Roman town planning. The triumphal arch was a Roman form much imitated in Renaissance and later architecture, often becoming an integral part of façade designs.
BELOW LEFT **S. Costanza, Rome**; *c.350*. Built as a mausoleum for the daughter of Emperor Constantine, this circular building became one of the works that carried the traditions of Roman architecture into the Middle Ages.

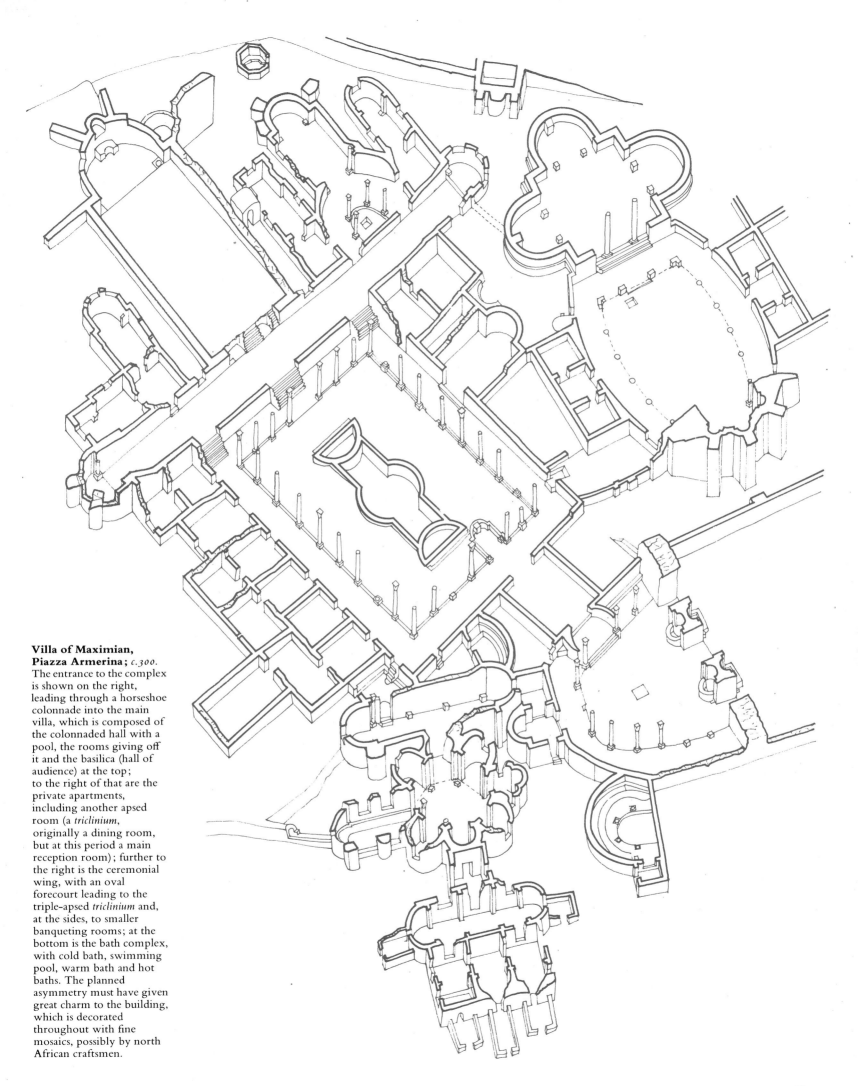

**Villa of Maximian,
Piazza Armerina;** *c.300.*
The entrance to the complex
is shown on the right,
leading through a horseshoe
colonnade into the main
villa, which is composed of
the colonnaded hall with a
pool, the rooms giving off
it and the basilica (hall of
audience) at the top;
to the right of that are the
private apartments,
including another apsed
room (a *triclinium*,
originally a dining room,
but at this period a main
reception room); further to
the right is the ceremonial
wing, with an oval
forecourt leading to the
triple-apsed *triclinium* and,
at the sides, to smaller
banqueting rooms; at the
bottom is the bath complex,
with cold bath, swimming
pool, warm bath and hot
baths. The planned
asymmetry must have given
great charm to the building,
which is decorated
throughout with fine
mosaics, possibly by north
African craftsmen.

29

CHAPTER 3

THE CHRISTIAN MIDDLE AGES

The monumental architecture of the Christian Middle Ages is devoted almost entirely to the church, the cathedral and other ecclesiastical buildings. The luxurious civilization of the Romans had been destroyed by invaders from the east and the north, and where monumental domestic buildings were erected they were strongly fortified; castles not villas were the rule. The early Christians had worshipped in private houses or secretly in catacombs, but with Christianity the established religion churches became public places, and as the powers of the Church gained ascendancy more and more care was lavished on the buildings. The church was the house of God and was the representation on earth of the heavenly city; it was the focal point of the medieval community from a tiny village to the Emperor's court.

Endless arguments were devoted to the correct liturgical form for a church, which had to serve both as a place for the priest's sacrifice and for congregational prayer, but in general it was orientated towards the east, and was built on the plan of a cross, either Greek (with four equal arms) or Latin (with one of the arms lengthened). The Greek cross allowed for a centrally-planned building and could make full use of both the square or the circle, while a Latin cross was derived from the basilica, the main nave being crossed towards the east end by a transept. As a landmark, to draw attention to the church, in western Christendom there was often a bell-tower or towers at the west end of the church, sometimes detached from the church building, sometimes towers at the end of the transepts, often a tower, lantern, spire or dome over the crossing. Orthodox churches could be roofed with a whole family of domes —one typical form, which evolved in the seventh century, having five, one over each arm and a larger one over the crossing. In addition, there might be a separate baptistery—particularly in the early centuries of Christianity, when the introduction of converts was one of the main church ceremonies—generally of circular form, following the Roman mausoleum. It is true that there is a great variety, but in some ways the form of the Christian church is as rigidly defined as was that of a Greek temple, and it was the dominant medium for architectural development for most of 1500 years.

The first buildings specifically intended as churches were built in the fourth century in Rome, mostly following the pattern of the basilica. The walls of the nave were carried on a colonnade, often making use of antique columns from pagan temples, topped either by the traditional straight entablature, or by little arches; the nave was covered with a wooden roof rather than a vault; there were one or occasionally two aisles on each side. The east end culminated in an apse, which would have the richest decoration, either wall painting or mosaic, to concentrate attention on this focal point in the church, and in some instances there is also a transept at the east end, giving the building the plan of a T.

OPPOSITE **Santa Sophia, Constantinople (Istanbul)**; *Anthemius of Tralles and Isidore of Miletus, 532–7.* The original Santa Sophia had been built by Constantine and the present building (converted to a mosque in the 15th century) dates from the reign of the Emperor Justinian. The illustration shows the extraordinarily bold way in which the dome is supported and the architects' great control of light in space.

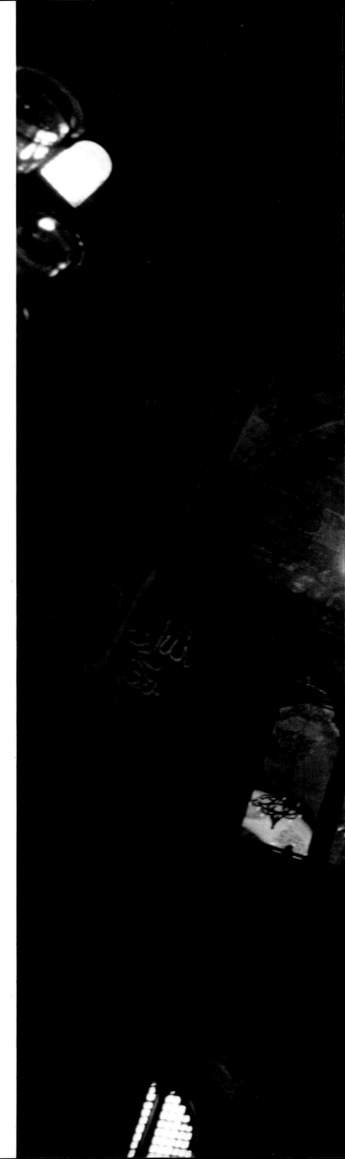

S. Maria Maggiore, Rome; *432–40.*
The Christian basilica was derived from the halls of justice of Imperial Rome, themselves a development from the covered markets of the Republican period. In the early basilican churches the vault was invariably avoided (it may have been considered a sign of pride), but in other respects S. Maria Maggiore is very close to its model in Roman architecture.

Outside Rome, the main centres of early church building were the provincial capitals of Ravenna in northern Italy, Constantinople, and Salonika in northern Greece. Santa Sophia in Constantinople, built for the Emperor Justinian, is a remarkable synthesis of the basilica scheme with the centrally planned church, since, although it has the equivalent of nave and aisles culminating in apses, the whole building is dominated by the immense dome over the centre of the nave, the first monumental example of a dome covering a square area, and the apses are covered with semi-domes, all pierced with windows, creating a rich luminous interior. The church was designed by two mathematician architects, Anthemius of Tralles and Isidore of Miletus, who were not only responsible for the technical achievement but also used correspondences of proportions to achieve a harmonious relationship between the spaces enclosed and the various elements which define and enclose them.

The other great foundation of Justinian was the church of S. Vitale in Ravenna, which is a more sophisticated version of the circular mausoleum-baptistery, a double octagon broken at the east end by the addition of an apse and with a porch added at the west. Its chief feature is the decoration with which the interior is covered, all strongly influenced from Constantinople (Byzantium):

richly carved capitals on the columns and in particular the magnificent mosaics, some of which depict Justinian, his Empress Theodora and their court.

While the Byzantine Empire grew in the east, the west was still beset by invasions and upheavals, and it was not until the end of the eighth century that there were signs of recovery. These came from the north, from the Frankish court of Charlemagne, which was to be established as the centre of a new 'Roman Empire'. The Emperor was responsible for many ecclesiastical foundations, and his octagonal mausoleum at Aachen was modelled directly on S. Vitale. Charlemagne's initiative was taken up by later Holy Roman Emperors, and during the tenth century large basilicas were built in the Rhineland and elsewhere in Germany, with a crossing at each end and a proliferation of towers, a form that survived into the eleventh and twelfth centuries. In other parts of northern Europe much of the building was in wood, which has remained only sporadically, as for example in the stave churches of Norway. Buildings such as the Carolingian gateway at Lorsch or the Saxon tower of Earl's Barton church in England, which are made of stone, appear to be related to wooden architecture, the thin bands of arcading being typical of wooden decoration.

LEFT **S. Vitale, Ravenna;** *526–48.*
The Byzantine interpretation of Classical architecture was very free, and full use was made of any element that could serve a decorative purpose, whether carved or covered with mosaics. The scene in the apse, visible between the columns, shows Justinian (who founded S. Vitale) and his court.

BELOW **Stave church, Vik, Norway;** *12th century.*
The Norwegian stave churches preserve some of the ancient traditions of the wooden architecture of northern Europe, which has its origins in pagan times. Elsewhere it is seen in only a few surviving examples throughout the continent—often in domestic buildings and in old farm buildings.

LEFT **Gate house, Lorsch;** *late 8th century.*
The lower part of the building is clearly derived from Roman models, but the flat decoration on the upper part seems to be related to a tradition of wooden architecture, although it incorporates Classical pilasters. The introduction of Classical elements into the much cruder local style is typical of Carolingian work.

RIGHT **Pantheon of the Kings, S. Isidoro, León;** *1054–7; painting 1175.* The painting on walls and vaults (part of a Last Supper scene is visible in the illustration) takes little account of the architectural form, but covers the surfaces with stylized figures, whose attitudes give a vivid account of the Christian stories.

After Charlemagne there was a period of increasing stability in Europe, coupled with a growth in the power of the Church. This brought with it the development of monastic communities dedicated to the service of God, which also served as repositories of learning. Communications between monasteries of the same Order were excellent—even over great distances—and this encouraged a greater internationalism of architectural styles to match the growing sophistication. Although there are strong regional variants, it is possible from the eleventh century onwards to talk of a Romanesque style throughout the continent of Europe. This was characterized by buildings based on simple geometric forms, with extensive use of the round arch; but the plainness of the architecture was relieved by the use of rich decoration. Interior surfaces were covered with wall-paintings; porches, columns, whole façades were decorated with sculpture and then painted too. Some of the finest wall-paintings are to be found in Spain, many in Catalonia, and in León, the 'Pantheon of the Kings', which had been the porch of the old basilica and contained more

S. Miniato, Florence; *1062 and 12th century.* Romanesque architecture reached one of its most refined forms in Tuscany, and the arcade with semi-circular arches and the geometrical division of the façade have led to the style being described as proto-Renaissance; S. Miniato is in fact composed of a Classical temple front placed over a broader front whose pediment it interrupts. The decoration of green and white marble, which was also to become a feature of Gothic architecture in Tuscany, is continued with even greater richness in the interior.

LEFT **Cathedral and Leaning Tower, Pisa;** *begun 1063 and 1174.* The cathedral façade is made up of similar elements to S. Miniato, but its proportions are less studied and the colonnades divide it up in a quite different way.

BELOW **Krak des Chevaliers;** *12th century* Double fortification walls and the provision of wells and food stores made the castle secure from attack and self-supporting over long periods of siege.

BOTTOM **Church of Paray-le-Monial;** *c.1100.* Paray-le-Monial was a priory of Cluny and closely imitated the style and forms, though not the vast scale, of St Hugh's church.

than forty royal tombs, now under the church of S. Isidoro, is a perfect example of Romanesque decoration, with richly carved capitals and the vaults of the ceiling covered with paintings of biblical scenes and Christian allegories.

A different form of ornamentation can be seen in Italy, where in the Florentine church of S. Miniato the decorative effect is achieved by the use of different coloured marble, both on the façade and on the wall areas of the interior. Similar decoration was also frequently used for the pavements of churches and with very rich elaboration for pulpits and other church furniture. Elsewhere in Italy, the decorative interest was created by the piling up of arcading on the exterior surfaces. One outstanding example of this is the cathedral at Pisa, which characteristically for Italy still has a separate bell-tower (the Leaning Tower) and circular baptistery.

Even as it became more stable, Europe was still prey to a strong sense of insecurity, and the cities and castles, which were developed were heavily fortified. This was strictly functional architecture and the immensely thick walls were not decorated in any way. European builders were in fact greatly indebted to Islamic fortifications, and it is fitting that perhaps the most impressive surviving castle of the Romanesque period should be the impregnable crusader castle of Krak des Chevaliers in Syria.

The crusades were in essence pilgrimages made to the tomb of Christ in Jerusalem, and during the early Middle Ages pilgrimage to the shrines of saints played a large part in the life of the Church. The prime inspiration came from the monasteries and in particular the reformed Cluniac movement, whose aim was to bring back a true sense of Christianity to monasteries, which had become very lax. The Benedictine Abbey of Cluny in Burgundy, from which the movement stemmed, was founded in the tenth century, and the second rebuilding of the church was begun by the abbot St Hugh at the end of the eleventh century. The Cluniac Benedictines believed that as the house of God the church should be as resplendent as human hands could make it, with a wealth of carving, painting and every sort of decoration, and they made the new church of their motherhouse the greatest church of the Middle Ages. Now, since Cluny was destroyed in 1810, we can only judge this from other churches of the Order, some of the finest of which are on the route of the pilgrimage to Santiago de Compostela in north-western Spain, which was sponsored by Cluny.

The Cluniac conception of the richly decorated church was fiercely attacked as luxurious and a sign of pride by St Bernard of Clairvaux, who in 1112 joined the new Cistercian Order. He demanded purity and simplicity in architecture as in all else, and Cistercian foundations throughout Europe built their churches in a most austere style and according to a standard plan.

The period around and just after 1100 was one of the most active for building in European history. In Germany the influence of Cluny was felt in the rebuilding of the great Rhineland cathedrals and abbeys, which still, however, retained their earlier form, with massive bulk and emphasis at both east and west ends. In England the period of greatest activity began about fifteen years after the Norman Conquest of 1066 and, although the Normans were quick to take over religious as well as secular administration, the Anglo-Norman style owes a great deal to its Anglo-Saxon background as well as to French influence. The extensive use of geometrical overall decoration, often in a way which tends to obscure the structure, is specially characteristic of the English, and the fact that this is more prevalent towards the end of the century suggests that a greater accommodation of the native population to their conquerors had taken place. As well as many parish churches and monastic buildings, almost all the great English cathedrals, which were also mainly of monastic origin, were started at this time, and nearly everywhere Romanesque portions, which were retained in later rebuildings, are still to be seen. The finest of those which are still fully Romanesque is Durham Cathedral, begun in 1093. In the nave there are three stages of arcading, the lowest one supported alternately by thick cylindrical columns with deep incised decoration and by piers made up of clusters of little half-columns, each corresponding to a part of the moulding they support. But the outstanding

RIGHT **Nave of Durham Cathedral**; *1093–1133*.

FAR LEFT Ste Madeleine, Vézelay; *1104–32, porch c.1120*.
One of the greatest Cluniac churches in Burgundy, Vézelay shows how effectively sculpture could be integrated into Romanesque architecture, often adding to the spirituality of the building, rather than creating a purely decorative effect.
LEFT St Sernin, Toulouse; *begun c.1080, completed 12th century, upper storeys of belfry 13th century*.
After Cluny itself St Sernin was the largest of the Cluniac churches, with five aisles in the interior and this proliferation of apses at the east end.
FAR LEFT BELOW Abbey of Maria Laach; *1093–1156*.
The abbey with its six massive towers follows the form of the great Rhineland cathedrals founded in the period of the Ottonian Emperors (863–1024), when Germany was at the forefront of European architecture. German Romanesque is often less richly decorated than contemporary architecture elsewhere in Europe.

RIGHT **Cathedral cloister, Monreale**; *1172–89*.
The successive conquests of Sicily led to a great mixture of styles, and while the paired columns and capitals of this Norman cloister show Byzantine influence, the pointed arches—an anticipation of Gothic—are certainly derived from the Moslems, who controlled Sicily from 827 to 1060.

feature of Durham is the vaulting, a great achievement of engineering which anticipates Gothic structures. Where there were not wooden roofs, churches had generally been covered either with a continuous half-cylindrical barrel-vault or with bays of groined vaulting —two short barrel-vaults intersecting at right-angles, to give an effect much like Durham without the ribs. These ribs are only decorative here, but they led to a system by which the pressure exerted by the vault was concentrated and supported at points of actual stress, so allowing much greater freedom in the treatment of the rest of the wall. This was fully exploited in Gothic buildings, which developed almost a skeleton construction, but Durham still remains the monumentality of Romanesque, though without the heaviness that was often found elsewhere. Another anticipation of Gothic styles is found in the architecture of the Norman conquerors of Sicily, where the extensive use of the pointed arch is derived from Islamic models.

Twenty years before the foundation of Durham another, very different, great church was completed: St Mark's in Venice, a city which had developed into an

RIGHT **St Mark's, Venice;** *dedicated 1073.*
St Mark's has the typical Byzantine Greek cross plan with five domes; the view here is taken from under the west dome towards the apse at the east end, and shows how richly the church is decorated.

ABOVE **Mosaic on the dome, Daphni;** *c.1080.*
Daphni was a sacred place on the road from Athens to Eleusis in Classical times, and the first Christian church was built there in the 5th or 6th century. The 11th-century mosaics exemplify the maturity of the 'classical' Byzantine tradition; Christ is represented as God and Judge descending from Heaven to judge good and evil.

important trading centre and had strong links, and rivalries, with Byzantium. In St Mark's the influence of Byzantine architecture is much more evident than that of the west, in the central planning, in the multiplication of domes and in the sumptuous carvings and mosaics in the interior, although the openness of the interior space, derived from Justinian's churches in Byzantium, had now become more typical of western architecture. In the Byzantine Empire itself, churches tended to be small and compact, and in the cities there were many churches and monasteries and countless chapels clustered together, as can be seen today among the ruins of Mistras in southern Greece. One of the larger Greek churches is the Katholikon at Daphni, decorated with superb mosaics, including the majestic figure of Christ the All-powerful on the dome. The interiors of Byzantine churches, often poorly lit and with paintings and mosaics of hieratic figures, have an air of great mystery, a sense of almost enveloping space. The eastern church also developed, more elaborately than in the west, and on three quite different levels, the symbolic functions of the church, and these were exemplified in the mosaics and paintings: its role as an image of earth and the Heavens, as a setting for the life of Christ on earth and as a concrete image of the liturgical year.

Throughout the Byzantine Empire developments of style were parallel, though with many local idiosyncrasies, particularly in the field of ornamentation. In what is now Yugoslavia a most expressive style of fresco painting was developed, while a group of late churches in Moldavia were decorated all over their exterior walls with narrative frescoes. More conventionally, as the interiors became more enclosed, the height of the churches was raised and there was a greater emphasis on verticality, stressed by the use of elaborate blind arcading, particularly in the churches of Byzantium itself. The domes, too, were lifted higher by elongating the drum on which they were supported. The cathedral of Mtskheta in Georgia demonstrates this squeezing upwards, showing too the almost complete absence of windows, which, by contrast, were to become such a dominant element in western churches. In metropolitan Russia the Byzantine style was first adopted at Kiev, but the major development took place further north at Novgorod, which escaped the Mongol invasions, and later around Moscow. Here too the vertical elements were stressed, and it was here that the characteristic 'onion' domes of Russia were introduced.

In the west the years around 1150 saw the beginnings of Gothic architecture, the essence of which lies in the development of the roof vault. More sophisticated methods of vaulting now allowed the whole construction to be supported not by solid walls but rather by a framework of stone, and with the discovery of the structural advantages of the pointed arch this technique was used with increasing daring as the Gothic

TOP LEFT **Painted exterior wall of St George, Voronet, Rumania;** *1547.*
One of a group of painted churches; the subject here —interrupted by a window —is the ancestry of Christ in the Tree of Jesse.

ABOVE **Mtskheta Cathedral;**
11th–15th centuries.
This cathedral in the former capital of Georgia is contained within a fortified enclosure; the church itself is composed of the simplest geometric elements, largely cubic blocks sliced at an angle to form the roofs, with a pattern of arcades superimposed. The style is typical of the Caucasus.

LEFT **Cathedral of St Dimitri, Vladimir;**
1193–7.
The rise of Vladimir as capital of northern Russia dates from the mid-12th century after the storming of Kiev (1169). The exterior of the cathedral has rich sculptural decoration, derived from wooden models.

RIGHT **Laon Cathedral;**
west front begun c. 1190.
Laon has the earliest and
best preserved Gothic
cathedral façade and
introduced many new
features that were to be
often imitated: the triple
porch, the rose window,
and the soaring towers, of
which seven were planned,
probably to be topped by
spires.
BELOW **Angel choir,
Lincoln Cathedral;**
begun 1256.
An example of mature
English Gothic with richly
carved arcading, rib vaults
and a window full of
patterned tracery.
BELOW RIGHT **Chapter
house, Wells Cathedral;**
begun 1285.
A canopy formed by the
thirty-two ribs from the
central column and nine
each from the eight corner
columns, typical of the
English taste for complex
abstract patterning.

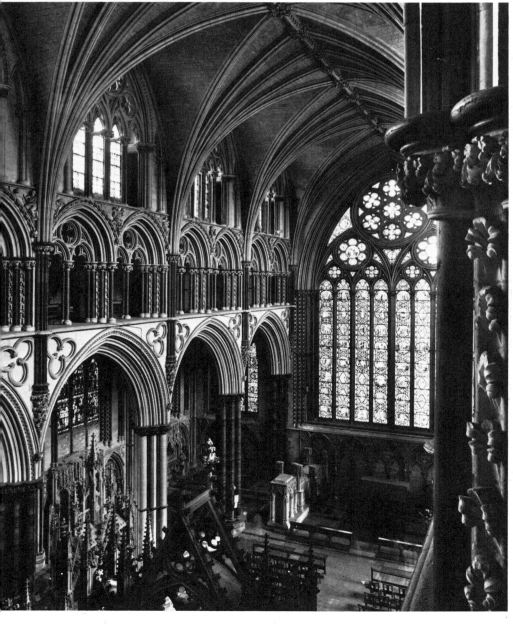

style evolved. Romanesque architecture had been firmly earthbound, with massive piers and towers, the round-topped arches always bringing the weight back to the ground; Gothic builders tried to bring their houses of God that much nearer God, to lift them off the ground and produce a truly spiritual architecture, made up more of void than of solid members. The most important single element contributing to this effect was the pointed arch, which strives upwards from both sides without the return to earth; at the same time, quite literally, it creates outward thrusts at the point where the arch springs, which need the support of buttresses. The characteristic open 'flying' buttresses can be seen in embryo in the earliest Gothic buildings, and on the exterior of the churches they too serve both to point upwards and to break up the flat walls, adding to the impression of insubstantiality created inside by the network of ribs on the vault, and by the walls, with their ever-increasing expanses of coloured glass. All these elements were integrated into a system of proportions derived from Classical architecture through Santa Sophia and the great Romanesque cathedrals, which meant that all the essential measurements of height, width and length are in harmonious simple arithmetical ratios.

Few of the great Gothic cathedrals were the work of a single architect, although the names of many master masons are known, and important achievements can be attributed to them; and probably none was designed and executed on the basis of one single set of plans. Even the greatest patrons, like Abbot Suger (1081–1151) who was responsible for the abbey church of St Denis, would seldom see their projects carried through to completion. Though each element was the work of an individual, the buildings as a whole were the result of an organic growth, often extending over several centuries. It is for this reason that it is not possible, as it is for later 'architect's' architecture, to isolate so simply the significant developments and chart the course of influences without a wealth of technical detail. But it is possible to see the course of general development from even a few significant examples: from the transition from Romanesque to Gothic in Chartres Cathedral, to the exuberant fan-vaulting of the chapter-house at Wells. Most of all, the effect of these great buildings has to be imagined in the context of their time—when ecclesiastical power far outstripped secular power—their tall towers and spires, even the high roofs above the naves, dominating the surrounding buildings, and the interiors filled with coloured light and reaching upwards to an unimagined height.

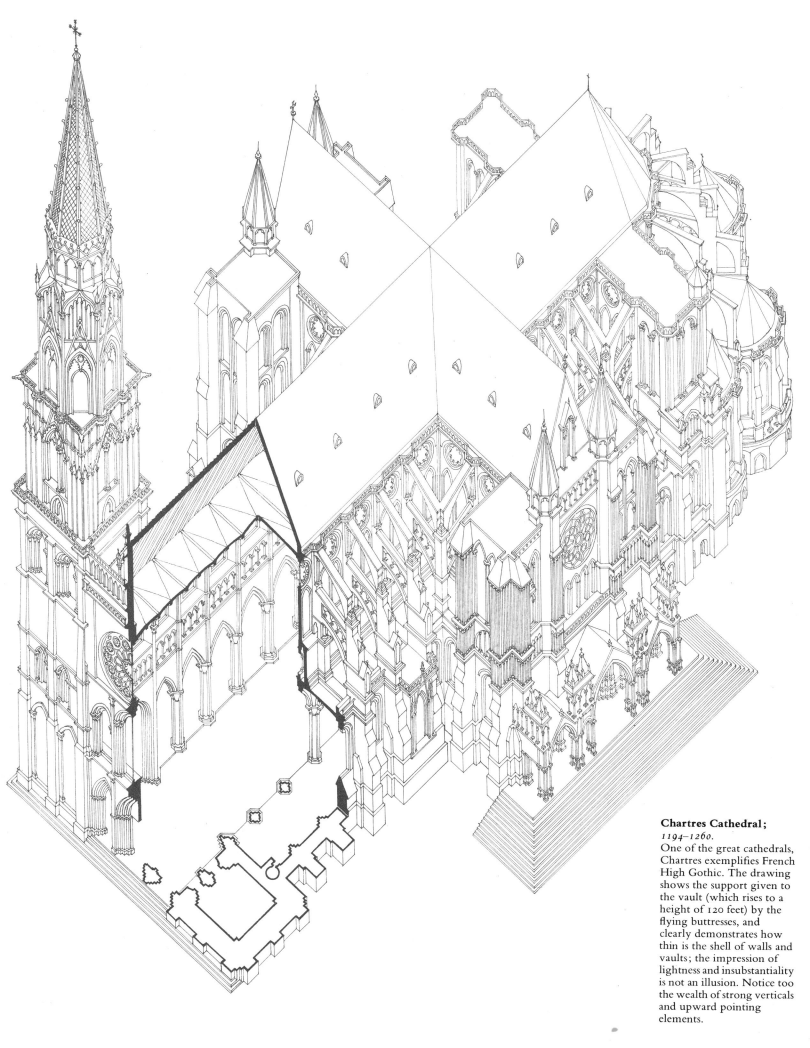

Chartres Cathedral;
1194–1260.
One of the great cathedrals, Chartres exemplifies French High Gothic. The drawing shows the support given to the vault (which rises to a height of 120 feet) by the flying buttresses, and clearly demonstrates how thin is the shell of walls and vaults; the impression of lightness and insubstantiality is not an illusion. Notice too the wealth of strong verticals and upward pointing elements.

TOP **Palazzo pubblico, Siena;** *1298.*
The tall towers of the palaces of medieval Italy were an assertion of pride by the powerful rival families and independent city states.

ABOVE **Vault of Lorenz-kirche, Nuremberg;** *begun 1439.*
The Lorenzkirche is expressive of the ambition and achievement of a great European trading city. Much fantasy is shown in the treatment of the ribs.

RIGHT **Jacques Coeur's house, Bourges;** *1442–53.*
This powerful merchant's house was exceptionally grand for the period and the decoration includes frequent reference to his name and coat-of-arms.

The greater stability of the later Middle Ages led to the rise in the importance of the towns. Increasingly, from the end of the thirteenth century, there is evidence in architecture of the rapidly expanding commerce both locally and with other towns, often over great distances. In northern Italy city states developed, and their civic hall (*palazzo pubblico*) on the main square or the market place was a focus for city life. The towns themselves had, meantime, grown up in a haphazard way, with no formal layout as in the Classical period, so that the important buildings—churches, civic buildings and town palaces of the rich or powerful—were built either on a square or piazza or fronting on one of the narrow streets; they still formed part of the unselfconscious organic growth of the environment.

Commerce brought wealth and this demanded ostentation, a demonstration that the wealth was there. This was achieved by an elaboration of the Gothic style, applied both to secular buildings and to the churches, which were enriched as the display-pieces of rival cities. Gothic forms lent themselves well to this elaboration, and each country—even city—developed its own local

variations. Many of these tended to emphasize the purely decorative elements, so that 'commercial' Gothic, though very pretty, sometimes loses touch with the origins of the style, which was essentially derived from constructional necessities, and so loses its strength. It is where the elaborate decoration goes hand in hand with new constructional feats that it is most successful. This was perhaps achieved most fully in England, where the technical mastery of the carpenters who constructed the hammer-beam roofs (like that of the masons who built the fan-vaults) is matched only by their fantasy in decoration.

At the time the carpenters were working on the roof at March there were already buildings standing in Italy designed in the new style of the Renaissance, based on pure geometric forms and with the minimum of decoration, yet Gothic still remained a living style until well after 1500. By this time, it is true, the forms had become very exaggerated, but some of the local variants are of great beauty. In England, this period saw the building of many of the finest spires and towers on the parish churches, some of the most elaborate wood-

PREVIOUS PAGE
St Wendreda, March, Cambs.; *c.1500.*
The roof at March is of double hammerbeam type, decorated at every possible join and in every space by angels with outspread wings. The rivalry of wealthy parishes (March and many of the East Anglian churches had been enriched by the wool trade) fostered a vernacular Perpendicular style, different from but not inferior to the grand Perpendicular of the cathedrals and court commissions (*see* p.7), with fine timberwork and tall towers and spires.

RIGHT **Detail of west front of St Maclou, Rouen;** *c.1500–14.*
One of the outstanding examples of Flamboyant Gothic, the actual structure is veiled by layer upon layer of filigree openwork, in which the asymmetrical flame shape is used which gave the style its name.

BELOW **Milan Cathedral;** *begun c. 1385.*
Building continued throughout the 15th century, and the façade was not completed until the 19th century (note the windows and doors which date from the Baroque age). The roof is a fantastic forest of pinnacles, but the underlying form, based on related triangles, is clearly expressed in the proportions of the façade.

working and, on a grander scale, the masterpieces of the 'Perpendicular' style, with their huge expanses of window and virtuoso fan-vaulting. At a later period this was even considered to be the 'national' style of England. The same was true of the 'Manueline' in Portugal, an even more elaborate version of Gothic, which introduced motifs of twisted and knotted ropes and many other features connected with seafaring in their great age of discovery. In France and Italy the late Gothic styles seem to have concentrated more on the proliferation of pinnacles and other decorative elements, giving an effect of great virtuosity, but perhaps appearing too elaborate and flimsy, at least to present-day taste.

Russo-Byzantine architecture reached its climax in Moscow with the walls, palaces and churches of the Kremlin, built in the half-century which spanned 1500, and based in conception on the Grand Palace at Byzantium. It gave representative form to Moscow's claim to be the new capital of the eastern Empire in succession to Byzantium, with the Tsars in direct succession to the Caesars. The palace incorporated into its Byzantine model both local elements derived from traditional wooden buildings and the work of Italian architects. Western influence was to become increasingly important in later Russian architecture, although this always remained an exotic strain within the main developments of the European Renaissance, and native traditions were never forgotten.

Church of the Deposition of the Virgin's Dress; gateway to Golden Room of the Tsarina, Kremlin, Moscow; *c.1485.*
Many churches were included among the palace buildings of the Kremlin as enlarged by Tsar Ivan III. This one, built by architects from Pskov, served as the private chapel of the Metropolitan of Moscow, and was connected by the stairs to the palace itself.

ABOVE LEFT **Window of the Convent of Christ, Tomar;** *Diogo de Arruda, 1510–14.*
The Manueline style in Portugal brought an extraordinary variety of natural motifs (many, like the ropes, chains and seaweed here, connected with the sea) to its decoration.
ABOVE **Lantern over crossing, Burgos Cathedral;** *Hans of Cologne, begun 1466.*
The Moorish tradition of covering vaults with intricate patterns is reinterpreted here in a Spanish cathedral by an architect experienced in the complex ribbing systems of German late Gothic.

CHAPTER 4

THE ISLAMIC ERA

The great religious art of Christianity had its parallel during the Middle Ages in the architecture of Islam. Soon after Mahomet's death in 632, Moslem dynasties had come to control the whole of the Middle East, and their world eventually extended from Spain in the west to Samarkand and India in the east, and southwards into Africa to the trading cities of the east coast and of the river Niger. Few of the dynasties were at all long-lived, but there is a unity to Islamic architecture created largely by the traditional form evolved for the mosque, the meeting place for prayer, and by the dictate which forbade the depiction of any living thing and was the cause of an unparalleled richness of abstract decoration.

The first Moslems of Arabia were from a nomadic people and the form given to the mosque can be thought of as oasis architecture: a rectangular courtyard with an enclosing wall with great gates, a tower to serve as a landmark, and inside a fountain, and at one end a hall. All the architectural interest is concentrated on what is inside the wall and, the gates apart, no great attention was paid to the exterior of the walls. The hall itself was generally colonnaded throughout, was lit by elaborately fretted windows, and had as its main features the *minbar,* or pulpit, and the *mihrab,* a niche in the wall which marks the direction of Mecca. But this was not nearly so strong an orientation as was the sacrificial altar at the east end of a Christian church, and the outstanding characteristic of the mosque was the use of rhythmical repetition of both architectural and, more particularly, decorative elements, which served to induce a state of contemplation in the worshippers. The decoration took the form of intricately intertwined patterns executed in wood, in stucco or in tiles, sometimes incorporating letters spelling out sentences from the Koran.

The form of the mosque shows clear evidence of the influence of Byzantine architecture, where equally the interior space was divided up, and attention was held by surface decoration, which nevertheless did not disguise the architectural forms. Byzantine influence on Islamic architecture was at first very strong, though this was combined with several other sources, in particular Hellenistic building and the ancient architecture of Persia and Mesopotamia.

The earliest surviving mosque is the Dome of the Rock in Jerusalem, originally a sanctuary built on the site of Mahomet's ascent into Heaven and of the old Jewish Temple. The mosque itself is here in the centre of the enclosure and was given its octagonal form in imitation of the already existing church of the Holy Sepulchre. Altogether it is one of the most obviously Byzantine of Islamic buildings, modelled on the round church or baptistery that in turn had its origin in Roman mausoleums, like the one which became the church of S. Costanza. A more characteristic example of the type is the Great Mosque at Damascus, built under the Ummayad dynasty, which has the tall minaret, the

OPPOSITE **Courtyard of mosque of Ibn Tulun, Cairo;** *c.868.*
The great courtyard with a fountain, which was always a standard feature of the mosque layout, goes back to the ancient semitic and Egyptian tradition of a precinct within which the temple stands, but it is also a conscious reflection of the layout of Mahomet's house at Medina. Pointed arches were a feature of Islamic architecture three centuries before they were introduced in western Europe. In the background can be seen the domes and minarets of the Muhamed Aly mosque, built in the 19th century in imitation of Santa Sophia in Istanbul.

arcaded courtyard and the great hall with interior colonnades entered on its long side. Like the Dome of the Rock, it was built on a sacred site and incorporates parts of earlier buildings.

One quite remarkable phenomenon of Islam was the rapidity with which it spread in the early years. The great mosque at Kairouan, in Tunisia, more than two thousand miles journey from Mecca, was started in 670, less than forty years after the death of Mahomet. Most of the existing structure dates from the time of the Abbasid caliphs in the ninth century. The interior of the arcade round the courtyard and the colonnades in the hall itself show an early example of the typical Islamic horseshoe arch lifted well above the capitals of the columns, while the arcade serves as a transition between the bright open sunlight of the courtyard and the obscurity of the interior of the hall. The arcades could also be a vehicle for decoration, as can be seen in the Ibn Tulun mosque in Cairo, the most important early Islamic building in Egypt, where there is elaborate stucco ornament laid over the brickwork, which would originally have been richly painted and gilt. Here too the fountain in the centre of the court, which is an essential part of the mosque complex, assumes greater importance, with a tall dome, dating from the thirteenth century, rising out of the square by means of an octagonal substructure and covering the octagonal basin.

Of all the early monuments of Islam, the one which most clearly shows its Middle Eastern origins is the Great Mosque at Samarra in Iraq, which was for a short

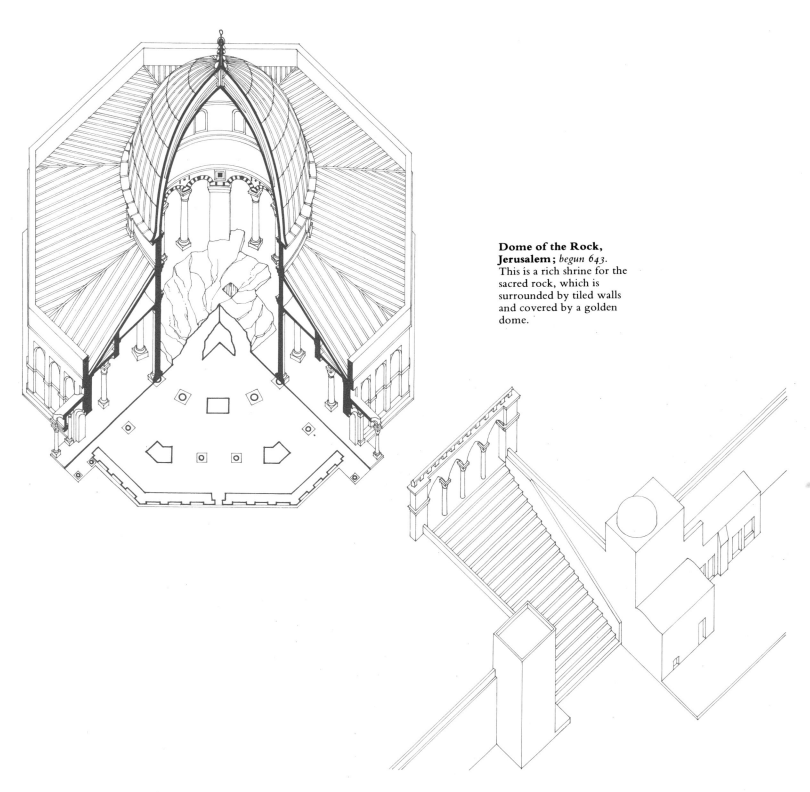

Dome of the Rock, Jerusalem; *begun 643.* This is a rich shrine for the sacred rock, which is surrounded by tiled walls and covered by a golden dome.

time the capital of the Islamic world. The most striking feature, apart from its huge size—it is the largest mosque in the world—is the spiral minaret, the *Malwiya,* built to a design that is derived from the ancient Babylonian *ziggurat* temple towers. These mosques show clearly the eclecticism of Islamic builders, for while the overall form remains fixed the structure of the various elements is derived from many sources. Early Islamic architecture was rootless, in that the original nomadic tribes in Arabia had no architecture at all, and they therefore borrowed whatever they found convenient.

The Ummayad dynasty, which had been overthrown by the Abbasids, was preserved in Spain, where they founded a capital city of Córdoba. The Great Mosque at Córdoba is one of the finest achievements of Islamic

FAR LEFT ABOVE
Ummayad mosque, Damascus; *705–15.*
The mosque stands on the site of the temple of Zeus, where a Christian church had been built in the 4th century. The square minaret was usual in the early years of Islam.
FAR LEFT BELOW **Malwiya minaret, Samarra;** *848.*
The minaret, built like the mosque of burnt brick, stands outside the great enclosure.
LEFT **Arcade of Great Mosque, Kairouan;** *9th century.*
The horshoe arches rest on antique columns taken from local Roman buildings.
BELOW **Minbar (pulpit), Sultan Hasan mosque, Cairo;** *1362.*
The mosque has a cross plan, with the fountain at the crossing and the central axis running from the *mihrab* through the centre of the very fine *minbar* (foreground).

RIGHT **Great Mosque, Córdoba**; *begun 786.* Successive enlargements in the 9th century quadrupled the area of the colonnade without essentially altering its form. The decorative effect is achieved by the use of stone and red brick.

BELOW **Hall of the Kings, Alhambra, Granada**; *second half 14th century.* View towards the fountain in the Court of the Lions. The foreground arches show typical Islamic 'stalactite' decoration, a combination of deep-cut hollows and little pendants.

BELOW RIGHT **Mosque, Jenne, Mali**; *14th century.* After the conquest of west Africa the trading cities on the upper Niger became important centres of Islamic culture. Their mosques show the sculptural and expressive qualities of mud architecture.

architecture, with internal colonnades of horseshoe arches with banded decoration, sometimes in two tiers and intersecting, which display great imagination. It is a forest of columns, the only comparison in Christian art being the Romanesque crypts under some of the great cathedrals, as at Canterbury or at Gurk in Austria. The decoration is still comparatively restrained at Córdoba, but it became increasingly exuberant and lavish, and the palace of the rulers of Granada, the Alhambra, which dates mainly from the thirteenth and fourteenth centuries, embodies all the decorative features of the western Islamic tradition in their most extreme form. The palace was, after the mosque, the most important structure in Islam, and was also a complex of buildings presenting a hostile exterior, but opening on the inside onto courtyards, and incorporating many halls, arcades and formal gardens with running water, symbols of the garden of paradise. At the Alhambra the depth of the arcades allows a great richness of interplay between light and shade, given still more variety by the light filtering through the fretted screens and the deep cutting of the stalactite arches. Every surface is covered with repetitive decoration, some of the bands incorporating elaborate script. It is hedonistic architecture unknown in Christian Europe until the masterpieces of Rococo in the eighteenth century.

Elsewhere in Spain, in the course of gradual Christian reconquest, many Moslem craftsmen remained and undertook work for their new masters, known as *mudéjar* work. One of the most impressive *mudéjar* buildings is the church of S. Maria la Blanca in Toledo, where the forms employed are all Islamic, although it was originally constructed in the twelfth century as a synagogue and was used for Christian, Moslem and Jewish worship. While the Moslems were on the retreat in western Europe and under pressure from the crusaders in the eastern Mediterranean, their missionary zeal had taken them far to the south, so that by the tenth and eleventh centuries they controlled trade from their traditional strongholds in the north African coastal territories across the Sahara to the Niger cities as well as the east-coast trade with India and China. In west Africa the architecture adopted the local techniques of mud building, but in the east more sophisticated stone mosques and palaces were erected, particularly in the later period, shortly before the destruction of the Islamic cities by the Portuguese 'explorers'.

In the east Islam saw a succession of rival dynasties. One of the longer lived was that of the Seljuks, whose origin was in Persia, where their massive brick structures underlie a number of the buildings of Isfahan, now covered with the brilliantly decorated tiles of a later era.

Citadel, Aleppo;
12th–14th centuries.
Syria, Lebanon and Palestine were the scene of constant warring with the crusaders and, often, with rival Islamic dynasties. The Moslems showed greater sophistication in their fortifications, though their lessons were soon learnt by the Christians (*see* p.35).

RIGHT **Double Minaret Madrasah, Sivas, Turkey;** *1271.*
Apart from the twin minarets (the bases of which can be seen) the gateway shows the typical Seljuk arrangement of stalactite decoration on a conical hollow within the outline of a pointed arch.

BELOW **Madrasah on Reghistan, Samarkand;** *begun 1420.*
Timur brought workmen from Persia to Samarkand, and the ribbed dome and cylindrical minaret—also covered in tiles—are characteristic Persian forms.

But the greatest surviving examples of Seljuk architecture are those of the Anatolian Seljuks from central Turkey. From their capital of Konya they built great fortified caravanserais, which were to protect travellers on the trade routes from the east. At Sultan Han, a royal foundation of the thirteenth century, the great court included, besides the mosque, accommodation for the merchants and, separately, for their attendants—who included resident musicians—a bath and stables. The architectural feature treated by the Seljuks with the greatest elaboration is the portal, and here the form is similar to the great Persian gateways, while the intricate carving on the stone is probably an imitation of tilework.

The Persians had always paid particular attention to the gateways of the mosque enclosure, which were built up much higher than the walls and hollowed out on the interior, sometimes so deeply that a semi-dome was almost created, with stalactite decoration. The

architectural forms remained nevertheless of great simplicity and the effect of richness was achieved by the brightly coloured tiles. In Persia everything was covered with tiles, and the most elaborate and brilliant examples of tiled architecture were created in Isfahan at the time of Shah Abbas, a contemporary of Queen Elizabeth I of England.

Two centuries earlier a strong Persian influence was to be seen further east along the silk route to China at Samarkand, the home city of the Mongol conqueror Timur, or Tamerlane. For the hundred years before its destruction in 1507, Samarkand became one of the great cities of Islam, and this is seen not only in the famous tombs of the royal family, but, as well, in the three great *madrasahs,* or colleges of learning, which flank the square of the Reghistan. Here, besides the decorative patterns and elaborate script, the tiles have—unorthodoxly—magnificent depictions of living creatures.

In Turkey yet another dynasty, the Ottoman, gained power, and it was they who made Islam's last incursion into Europe, taking Constantinople in 1453 and leaving the influence of their culture in many of the Balkan countries before their final defeat after the unsuccessful siege of Vienna in the late seventeenth century. The sixteenth century was their golden age and their architecture is dominated by the work of Mi'mar Sinan (1489–1578/88), royal architect for over thirty years. His greatest work was the mosque of Selim II at Edirne (Adrianople). Taking Santa Sophia—which was now converted for use as a mosque—as a model, he made a single unified interior space covered by a dome; but the enormous dome (103 feet in diameter) is raised higher than in the Byzantine building on an octagonal structure, enabling Sinan to create a yet more imposing and unified exterior, which is completed by the four towering corner minarets.

LEFT **Mihrab of Shaikh Lutfullah mosque, Isfahan;** *1602–19.*
Shah Abbas's greatest project was the construction of the buildings around the vast Royal Quadrangle, used as a polo ground. The Shaikh Lutfullah mosque was the first to be completed, followed by the Shah mosque and the Ali Kapi palace. The tiled and tile mosaic decoration of the mosques is of exquisite beauty.

ABOVE **Selim mosque, Edirne;** *Sinan, 1568–74.*
The placing of the four minarets ensures that the dome becomes the focal point of the building, although it is not at the centre of the whole mosque complex. It is understandable that in the heart of the former Byzantine empire Byzantine architecture should have been far more influential than Islamic styles.

53

The last of the great Islamic civilizations was that of the Moghul dynasty in India which reached its highest point in the second half of the sixteenth century, during the reign of Akbar the Great. Delhi had fallen to the Moslems in 1192, and from that time Islam had become an increasingly potent force throughout northern India, although the famous Kutb-i-minar minaret in Delhi is one of the very few early Islamic monuments extant there. From the first, Persian influence had been predominant, and with the arrival of the Moghuls, whose origin was Samarkand, this became stronger still, although it was mingled with the effect of Afghan architecture and there were many specifically Indian elements which radically changed its character. In particular, the simple geometric forms with their decoration of tiles were enlivened with pinnacles, pavilions and far more exuberant ornamentation, derived originally from the richly sculptured Hindu temples, and the tiles themselves were replaced with carving in the building stone or with inlay or mosaics of coloured marbles. The masterpiece of Islamic art in India is Akbar's palace at Fatehpur Sikri, built in pink sandstone. Its basic form is one that is already familiar from traditional Islamic buildings, but its detailing is of great originality and invention. Akbar's successors refined the style, often employing very costly materials, and devoting much of their energies to elaborate tombs, which are practically palaces for the dead; the most famous and the most splendid of these is the Taj Mahal. The finest of the late Islamic buildings in India retain the vigour of their models and in their form still proclaim their origins in the oasis architecture of the nomads.

Taj Mahal, Agra; *1632–53.*
This funerary monument
to the wife of Shah Jahan is
the perfection of Moghul
art. The building's purity of
form is heightened by its
being constructed entirely
of marble and by its setting
in spacious formal gardens.
Although it has been
variously attributed to the
Venetian Geronimo
Verroneo and to two sons
of a pupil of the Turkish
architect Sinan, it is almost
certainly the work of
Moghul architects and
craftsmen.

BELOW **Palace Garden,
Amber;** *17th century.*
The palace fort of Amber
was built by the Hindu
Maharajahs Man Singh I
and Jai Singh I, who were
closely associated with the
Moghul emperors. The
garden, by an artificial lake,
shows the complete
absorption of Islamic
features into Indian
architecture, in the varied
patterns of the beds, the
octagonal pool and the
central canal.

CHAPTER 5

THE RENAISSANCE

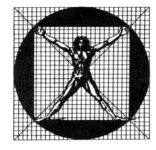

The Renaissance was a period not so much of rebirth as of revival, a conscious attempt to look back beyond the immediate past to the Classical age of Greece and Rome. The Reformation, which sought a return to the roots of Christianity, was a part of this movement and was particularly significant in the countries of northern Europe, and the same spirit of revival, in many different forms, invaded every field of the arts. In architecture its obvious characteristics are the use of simple geometrical forms, based largely on the circle and the square, and the use of the Classical Orders both structurally and for decoration.

Like the discovery of linear perspective, which marks the real beginning of the Renaissance in painting, the new architecture began in Florence with the work of the goldsmith Filippo Brunelleschi (1377–1446). In 1420 he started work on the dome which was to complete Florence Cathedral, and this was finished fifteen years later. He was still using the Gothic idiom, which harmonizes with the rest of the cathedral complex, but already the interior of this huge dome, an extraordinary feat of engineering, is designed with a sense of handling great masses of space harmoniously. It is as if the space contained has assumed equal or even greater importance than the shell containing it. The rediscovery of architectural space is the greatest achievement of Renaissance architecture, and although it needed a reversion to Classical forms and Classical simplicity to achieve it, these were only a means to an end, and the buildings of the early Renaissance were developments not imitations of Roman architecture, drawing as well on the local Tuscan Romanesque tradition, exemplified in the Florentine church of S. Miniato.

A year before starting on the dome of the cathedral, Brunelleschi had begun work on the cloisters of the Foundling Hospital, considered to be the first building in the Renaissance style. This and all his major works are characterized by the simple mathematical ratios between the various elements, the use of round arches supported on Classical columns, and the clear articulation of the surface by contrasting the colour of the stone used for the columns and mouldings with that of the plaster of the wall surfaces. Brunelleschi had been to Rome to sketch and measure the circuses, temples, basilicas and baths of Antiquity, and it was on these that the theorists of the Renaissance based their ideas, and on the one architectural treatise to have survived from the ancient world. This was the work of the Roman military engineer and architect Vitruvius (active 46–30 BC). His *De Architectura* is in fact a rather garbled piecing together of a number of—sometimes conflicting—Greek architectural theories, with other chapters derived from his own experience of engineering and construction techniques. Even today no scholar has satisfactorily sorted out the different sources he used and what is the real meaning of all that he wrote.

OPPOSITE **Courtyard of Foundling Hospital, Florence;** *Brunelleschi, designed 1419, built 1421–44.* In contrast to the elaboration of Gothic architecture, Renaissance classicism frees the vision as much as possible, by making use of forms of the utmost clarity. Brunelleschi employed the Classical Orders to achieve this, though his handling of them differed in many ways from that of Antiquity: whereas the Greeks and Romans would only use columns to support a flat entablature, in a strict post and lintel construction, Brunelleschi had his columns supporting arches, making them part of a solid masonry wall—as had been the practice of Romanesque architects and before them the Byzantines. Early Renaissance styles were as much part of a continuing tradition as a great leap back over more than a thousand years.

BELOW **Study of Duke Federigo Montefeltro, Ducal Palace, Urbino;** *attributed to Bramante and Francesco di Giorgio, c. 1475.* The decorations in inlaid wood show how effectively false perspectives can give an illusion of real space. The geometry of linear perspective held a fascination for Renaissance architects.

RIGHT **Pazzi Chapel, Florence;** *Brunelleschi, 1429–44.* The simple geometric forms emphasize the linear quality of Brunelleschi's designs.

BOTTOM RIGHT **Rucellai palace, Florence;** *Alberti and B. Rossellino, 1446–51.* Alberti copied the Roman Colosseum, where the three stages are distinguished by rows of half-columns in each of the three Orders, but used shallow pilasters, which are better suited to the flat palace façade.

Renaissance scholars did not try to. They swallowed Vitruvius whole and he became the architects' bible.

Apart from the definition of the Orders, the most important gift to the Renaissance from the Classical world, via Vitruvius, was the theory of proportions. Man was the measure, so that all dimensions were related to the human scale—something that fitted in very well with current humanistic thinking—and all dimensions were related to one another in simple arithmetical proportions. Leon Battista Alberti (1404–72) was chiefly responsible for the formulation of early Renaissance architectural theory, basing his *Ten Books on Architecture* on Vitruvius, on his knowledge of Classical buildings and on the new way of building developed earlier in the century by his fellow Florentines. The *Books* covered a very wide range of subjects, from history, siting, design, construction, town-planning and engineering to sociology, the philosophy of beauty, perception and perfection. This treatise by Alberti, a dilettante not an architect by profession, did much to establish architecture, till then considered a mere trade, on a par with the other fine arts. No complete building of Alberti's survives intact and several of his works involved the completion or 'modernization' of old-fashioned buildings. He incorporated a pedimented temple front in his design for a new façade for the Florentine church of S.

Maria Novella—destined to become the prototype of Renaissance façade to a basilican church and enormously influential for several centuries. This was built under the patronage of the rich merchant family of the Rucellai, and he had also designed Giovanni Rucellai's town palace, which followed a pattern, set earlier in the century in the Medici palace designed by Michelozzo, of a flat three-storey façade with rusticated stonework, well protected against enemies in this age of violent family feuding, and with the main reception rooms on the *piano nobile*, above the ground floor. Alberti introduced a new element, replacing the graded rustication, which had been used previously to distinguish the three floors, with flat pilasters that flank the windows on each storey and, in imitation of the Colosseum, incorporate the three Orders, Doric, Ionic and Corinthian, from bottom to top.

Alberti was the apostle who took Renaissance architecture from Florence to the rest of Italy. Not only did he undertake buildings in Rimini and Mantua, using a monumental style closely following Classical Roman models and more consciously three-dimensional than Brunelleschi's, but for a time he shared supervision of building at the Vatican in Rome during the pontificate of Nicholas V, who had initiated a great programme for the rebuilding and renovation of the city. Rome

now became a magnet to artists and architects as work got under way and it saw the realization of the theories and ideals of the Florentine Renaissance. In 1452 Alberti had presented his treatise to the Pope, who thereupon shelved the plans he had already had prepared for consolidating and embellishing old St Peter's and rebuilding the choir, and the complete reconstruction of the basilica became the greatest architectural undertaking of the Renaissance, involving every pope and numerous architects for two centuries. The most significant step was taken by Pope Julius II, who in 1505 commissioned Donato Bramante (1444–1514) to design a new church.

Bramante came from Urbino, and one of his earliest works was the completion of the Gothic church of S. Maria delle Grazie in Milan. After Milan was invaded in 1499 by the French, he too went to Rome and in 1502 was commissioned by Ferdinand and Isabella of Spain to undertake a little temple (*Tempietto*) in the cloister of S. Pietro in Montorio in Rome. The *Tempietto* is the realization of the concept of a circular church, whose abstract perfection had been praised by the Renaissance theorists, and is an adaptation of the Classical circular temple as a Christian shrine. Like the church in Milan, the effect of harmony and equilibrium, of space enclosed rather than the enclosing structure, is achieved by extreme simplicity and by the practical application of the rules of proportion which had been formulated by Alberti. Bramante's buildings are the most perfect embodiment of Renaissance theory. His design for St Peter's was an elaboration of the design of the *Tempietto*; it was centrally planned with a huge dome over the crossing and four equal arms each terminating in a semi-dome over a portico. Between each arm was to be a tower. Work started according to Bramante's plan, but after his death and that of his patron construction stagnated until Michelangelo (1475–1564) was appointed architect of St Peter's in 1546.

Once Alberti had established the respectability of architecture, many of the greatest artists of the period had had works commissioned from them, and Raphael too undertook palaces in Rome, completed Bramante's great loggia in the Vatican Palace and was for a time engaged on St Peter's. Michelangelo's important work as an architect had begun with a chapel to contain tombs of the Medici family in Brunelleschi's S. Lorenzo in Florence. Although he retained the simple Classical pilasters and semi-circular arches in grey stone against whitewashed stucco that had characterized Brunelleschi's work, Michelangelo broke the canons of Classical proportions by raising the dome over the square room much above its 'correct' height and dividing the wall areas into three horizontal zones. The integration of sculpture—notably his figures of Day and Night—in the lowest zone and the richness of light in the highest foreshadow the sculptured decoration and the theatrical use of light that came to distinguish Baroque architecture from the spatial equilibrium of the Renaissance. The same characteristics are to be seen in the Laurentian Library in Florence and the Palazzo Farnese in Rome, in which Michelangelo had a decisive hand. His plan for St Peter's followed the essential elements of Bramante's plan, but the simplifications he introduced produced a more massive sculptural effect, and by abandoning the conventional use of the Orders, which had served to distinguish the storeys and to relate all dimensions to the human measure, in favour of giant pilasters, Michelangelo made the decisive break with Renaissance tradition. The centralized plan for St Peter's was in the end abandoned in favour of the Latin cross, and the basilica as it stands today is much changed from Michelangelo's project, but his is nevertheless the greatest single contribution to the building.

LEFT **Tempietto, Rome;**
Bramante, 1502.
This is the archetypal round church of the Renaissance, an expression of human harmony as an echo of divine harmony. Alberti has laid down that it should be built in the centre of a beautiful square, free on all sides and placed on a high platform to isolate it from surrounding buildings, its dome a perfect hemisphere.
BELOW **St Peter's, Rome;**
Bramante, Michelangelo and others, begun 1506.
The monumental simplicity of the *Tempietto* was reflected in Bramante's design for St Peter's, and made grander by Michelangelo's use of the colossal Order—pilasters carried up through two storeys. This view gives an idea of the church as planned, before the elongation of the nave.

Before working on St Peter's, Michelangelo had been appointed architect-in-chief of the papal palaces, and his understanding of large-scale architectural design can be seen in his remodelling of the Roman Capitoline Hill, the Campidoglio. In a masterly way he changed a jumble of buildings on top of a hill, approached by irregular footpaths, into an ordered square, which remains one of the most impressively beautiful in the world. The piazza is reached up a flight of ramped steps, flanked at the top by massive antique statues of Castor and Pollux, protectors of Rome. The focus of the square is the statue of Marcus Aurelius (also a traditional symbol of Roman law and government), which is set at the centre of an oval decorated in a star pattern, of cosmic significance. To left and right two identical palaces, one new, one an old building refaced, converge towards the Palace of the Senator which closes the square, again an old building refaced by Michelangelo and integrated to the flanking structures by its grandiose staircase. The origins of Michelangelo's designs for all these buildings in recent Renaissance tradition is obvious, and yet his deployment of the elements is utterly different. For Brunelleschi and Bramante the human scale was of supreme importance, but Michelangelo has massive

pilasters on the façades of the palaces rising through two storeys. The exaggeration of scale, the use of distorted geometrical forms (oval and trapezoid), the dramatic use of sculpture, and above all the whole theatrical effect both as the visitor approaches the square and then is enveloped in it—these are elements which typify the environmental planning of the later Baroque age.

Although Michelangelo's architecture is carried out with such firm purpose and stringency, his departures from the Renaissance norms are seen as the beginning of 'Mannerism', a term originally used to describe the more wilfully mannered derivatives of the Classical Renaissance style. The most influential of the Italian Mannerist architects was Raphael's pupil Giulio Romano (1499–1546), who was the creator of a highly individual work in the country villa of the Dukes of Mantua, the Palazzo del Té. His use of Classical language in a way which deliberately offends against Classical canons of proportion is not, as in Michelangelo's architecture, part of a grander sculptural design, but serves to create a novel decorative effect by its very perversity, essentially structural elements such as columns and pediments, rustication, etc., being used without any real structural purpose.

Campidoglio, Rome;
Michelangelo and others, begun 1539.
The Palace of the Senator at the end of the square and the two flanking palaces were remodelled, largely following Michelangelo's designs, in the latter part of the 16th century. They are related both by the use of the colossal Order and by Michelangelo's brilliant spatial conception: the convergence of the sides of the square leads the eye along the side palaces to the building at the end, almost as in a stage set, while the oval pattern on the pavement—the first use of the oval in Renaissance architecture —draws the buildings closer together, creating an effect of one space contained within another.

The use of 'Mannerism' has been extended to include those other Italian architects who, without the wilfulness of Giulio Romano, had followed Michelangelo in departing from the extreme clarity of early Renaissance architecture to create a more monumental effect. All of the three most important of these—Serlio, Palladio and Vignola—also wrote architectural treatises, which, in conjunction with their actual buildings, were to have great influence for a century and more. Sebastiano Serlio (1475–1554) belonged to the earlier generation, and his importance lies chiefly in the inspiration given by his treatise (particularly its illustrations) in France, where towards the end of his life he was called to the court of Francis I at Fontainebleau. This was the centre of Mannerism in France, and the king's château was decorated with paintings and stucco, in imitation of the work of Raphael and Giulio Romano in Rome and at the Palazzo del Té, by the Italian artists Primaticcio (who had worked with Giulio) and Rosso.

Andrea Palladio (1508–80) was the greatest architect of his age. His work is the reverse of the Mannerist coin; although Classical motifs and structures are employed with more freedom than by the architects of the early Renaissance, they are handled with great strictness with regard to proportion. In his grand churches in Venice, S. Giorgio Maggiore and the Redentore, the piling of columns and pediments up to the domes can seem dull, but his villas on the Brenta river on the mainland are models of Renaissance principles applied to domestic architecture. Palladio went back again to Vitruvius and Classical Antiquity and many of his interpretations were taken as models by generations of succeeding architects. All his villas are symmetrically planned with rigorous geometry, sometimes including rooms of single- or double-cube proportions. A recurring feature is the arcade of columns set right forward from the main wall of the house, whether as a portico or a loggia, which serves to relate the building to its immediate surroundings, by blunting the impact that a plain wall would have, while his use of statues on the skyline also serves to break the definition of the roof-line. Although the language of Palladio's architecture is rooted in the past and in a rigidly intellectual approach to his material, his handling has a strongly theatrical element which links him closely with the following generation of Baroque architects; not only in his ability to design a building with a strong sense of its setting, but also in the way in which his

buildings increasingly involve the spectator, the flights of steps, the arcades, drawing him in and blurring the distinction between the outside world and the stage the architect has set.

Giacomo Vignola's (1507–73) most important work was the mother-church of the newly founded Jesuit Order, the Gesù in Rome. This was a new attempt to combine the traditional medieval church plan with the Renaissance ideal of a centrally planned church. The nave is wide, covered by a tunnel vault, and above the crossing is a large dome which gives the central focus; the aisles are converted into little side-chapels off the nave. The façade (which was not built according to Vignola's plan, but was based upon it) provides a new solution, derived from Alberti's S. Maria Novella in Florence, to the problem of adapting Classical language to the scheme of a broad lower storey and a narrower top storey, by joining them with large curved scrolls or volutes. Many of these elements were used with variations by later Baroque architects, and the scheme of the Gesù was more frequently copied and adapted than any other church plan of the whole Renaissance period.

ABOVE LEFT **Villa Foscari, Malcontenta;** *Palladio, c.1560.*
Palladio believed, quite wrongly, that the pedimented temple front was used in domestic architecture in Classical times, and his huge porticos approached by steps, which were universally imitated, represented his conception of a Roman villa.

ABOVE RIGHT **Palazzo del Té, Mantua;** *Giulio Romano, 1526–31.*
This was also an attempt to recall the villas of Imperial Rome. Giulio had worked with Raphael on the Villa Madama in Rome, but here he made freer use of Classical language, to create a highly theatrical effect.

Royal staircase (formerly chamber of Mme d'Etampes), Fontainebleau; *c.1541–5.*
Interior decoration with frescoes and rich stuccowork was first developed by Raphael and Giulio Romano, but reached its fullest elaboration in the work of the Italian artists at the court of Fontainebleau. Most influential of these was Francesco Primaticcio (1540/5–70), who worked with Giulio at the Palazzo del Té and who executed the sculpture and most of the paintings in the room illustrated. The staircase and ceiling are 19th-century.

RIGHT **Detail of carved gateway, Salamanca University;** *c.1525–30.* All the detailing is based on Renaissance patterns (the 'grotesque' ornament being derived from the painted decoration of Ancient Rome), but the form shows no trace of the Classical Orders or Renaissance systems of proportion. The design is an allegorical tribute to Ferdinand and Isabella: a roundel with their double portrait is contained in the lowest band, while the upper bands, carved in increasingly deep relief, show coats-of-arms, busts of Adam and Eve, and a papal scene attended by Hercules and Venus.

Outside Italy, particularly in those countries most affected by the Reformation, the traditional Gothic styles persisted well into the sixteenth century, and it was the new Classical decoration, rather than the structural ideas, that began to come into use and that chiefly in domestic buildings. In France, even before the strongly Manneristic architecture of the Palace of Fontainebleau, Italian artists and craftsmen had been at work in a number of places, and many Frenchmen became familiar during the wars of the first two decades of the sixteenth century with the new buildings in northern Italy. This was a period of intense architectural activity in France, particularly on the rival châteaux on the river Loire, but even where Italian masons were working, as at Chambord, the structure remains essentially medieval, though the ornament is of the Renaissance.

Spain's contribution to Renaissance architecture had begun early on with Ferdinand and Isabella's commission of the *Tempietto* from Bramante—in its own way as significant as their support for Columbus. But in Spain itself the 'Isabelline' style of the first decades of the six-

Garden front, Château of Chambord; *begun 1519.* Here Italian workmen were employed and the influence of the Renaissance can be seen not only in the huge symmetrical plan, but also in the clear articulation of the three storeys, which incorporate Classical pilasters. The horizontal emphasis and the ordered classicism are countered by the exaggerated verticals of the roofs and chimneys, which still show clearly their Gothic derivation, although decorated largely with Renaissance motifs.

teenth century is characterized by large areas of stone-work decorated with overall shallow relief, known as 'plateresque' (silversmiths') work. It is in many ways equivalent to the contemporary Manueline work in Portugal, but while that remains a highly idiosyncratic version of Gothic, Isabelline architecture is not only indebted to the intricate overall decoration of the Moors, but also contains many elements of Renaissance detailing. One of the finest examples is the façade of the University of Salamanca, with medallions, coats-of-arms and grotesques.

The same preoccupation with decoration is evident in the Low Countries and Germany, where the Reformed church viewed Italianate styles with great disfavour. In Antwerp, which had also developed its own individual style of Mannerist painting, a new decorative style was originated making much use of 'strapwork'—patterns of elaborately interlacing scrolls and straps moulded in plaster or carved in shallow relief. This was derived in part from the decorations at Fontainebleau and from Serlio's treatise, and was to become one of the main elements of Renaissance decoration in northern Europe.

The work at Fontainebleau had a decisive effect and encouraged native French artists to develop a Renaissance style of their own. The most important architect was Philibert Delorme (c. 1510–70), trained in Rome and appointed court architect to Francis I's successor Henri II. Together with Jean Bullant (c. 1520–78) he built the new Tuileries Palace in Paris, which was of far-reaching influence. But the palace was destroyed during the Commune in 1871 and Delorme's surviving masterpiece is the château at Anet, designed for Henri's mistress Diane de Poitiers. This includes in its plan a domed centrally-planned chapel, and the entrance pavilion to the château makes use of Classical motifs with extreme freedom, but combines them with pierced balconies derived from the Gothic tradition. These are also to be seen, in a Gothic context, in the church of St Etienne-du-Mont in Paris (see p. 10).

In England, after the dissolution of the monasteries by Henry VIII, there was more destruction than erection of ecclesiastical buildings, but in the universities of Oxford and Cambridge fully Gothic buildings were put up throughout the sixteenth and well into the seventeenth century. At the same time, the greater stability of Tudor rule led the new nobility, many enriched with confiscated monastic lands, to build country houses—no longer fortified castles as in medieval times, but grand buildings reflecting the more sophisticated taste of the age. Increasingly, Italian influence was felt. Not only were many Italian masons, plasterers and other craftsmen employed, but workmen from the Low Countries also introduced their own individual type of Renaissance decoration. Sir John Thynne's Longleat House shows how Renaissance principles of proportion could be applied to an English country house, though he makes very limited use of the Classical Orders.

In the reign of Elizabeth I, the architecture became more extravagant, and Robert Smythson (c. 1536–1614) at Wollaton makes Manneristic use of medieval, Italian and Flemish Renaissance motifs, while Hardwick Hall (also attributed to Smythson) retains a symmetrical plan, but is built up of storeys of brickwork with vast expanses of glass windows, the storeys not articulated by Classical Orders but by their differing proportions. Here the lessons of Renaissance architecture have been learnt, but appear in an entirely different language from that of Michelangelo or Palladio.

The High Renaissance in Spain and Portugal (temporarily united under Philip II) is characterized by a severe and monumental ecclesiastical style. This was

LEFT **Entrance pavilion, Château of Anet;** *P. Delorme, c.1552.* Here the forms are fully Classical, but are used with great freedom; the interplay of the volumes which go to make up the gatehouse is complex but effective, and characteristic of French architecture. The pierced balconies served for the ladies to watch the departure and return of the hunt.

ABOVE **Longleat House;** *Sir John Thynne, Robert Smythson master mason, completed 1572.* This was the first great Elizabethan house to show fully the influence of French and Italian styles. There are many resemblances to Chambord—the symmetrical plan, the windows flanked by pilasters and the strong horizontal bands—but the flat planes of the façade, with a very high proportion of window to wall, are more restrained and more typically English.
LEFT **Egeskov Castle, Denmark;** *Martin Bussert, begun c. 1545.* Although Bussert pioneered Renaissance styles in Denmark, this is apparent at Egeskov only in the rounded arches and clearly defined proportions of the brick walls; but the fortification still served defensive purposes and was not purely ornamental.

TOP **South façade, Escorial;** *J. B. de Toledo, 1562–7.*
Philip II's vast palace-monastery was designed on a strict grid plan with the church (a Greek cross plan in a square) and a great court on the axis, and equal square areas devoted to palace and seminary on the north, monastery and formal garden on the south. The south façade and the garden were the only parts completed before Toledo's death.
ABOVE **Mauritshuis, The Hague;** *J. van Kampen and P. Post, begun 1633.*
RIGHT **Château of Balleroy;** *François Mansart, 1626–36.*
Mansart achieved balance and harmony without any recourse to the Orders, by studied proportions, clear articulation with stone of two colours, and an equilibrium of vertical and horizontal elements.

derived from Italian Mannerism and was well suited to the early years of the Counter-Reformation, which saw the rise of the Jesuit Order and the terrifying operation of the Spanish Inquisition. Vignola's Gesù was imitated early on by Jesuit churches in the three Portuguese cities of Lisbon, Coimbra and Évora, but the greatest monument in this style is Philip's vast royal palace-monastery of the Escorial. This was built by Juan Bautista de Toledo (d. 1567) and Juan de Herrera (c. 1530–97) and embodies the chill use of the Classical Orders in a rigid symmetrical plan. Although more monastery than palace, it was nevertheless the first of the really large-scale royal buildings in Europe and set a standard which many later monarchs felt they had to emulate.

Early in the seventeenth century fully developed Renaissance styles reached northern Europe, and the work of the English architect Inigo Jones (1573–1652) is strongly Italianate, imitating in particular the work of Palladio. At the Queen's House at Greenwich (*see* p. 70) he used a curving staircase and a simple finely proportioned façade topped by a balustrade, while his Banqueting Hall in Whitehall (designed as the beginning of a grandiose new palace for Charles I, of which only this was built) makes use of rustication and pilasters and columns on the façade, which is clearly derived—via Palladio—from the earliest town palace façades of Florence. The strict application of Palladian geometry to the proportions of his interiors was characteristic of Jones's work, and the famous single- and double-cube rooms at Wilton House, which also make decorative use of Renaissance ornament, are examples of fully Italianate work in England.

Similar developments were to be seen in Germany, where the outstanding work is Augsburg Town Hall by Elias Holl (1573–1646), and in Holland. Here the amateur architect Jacob van Kampen (1595–1657) built the monumental Amsterdam Town Hall and some years earlier, in conjunction with Pieter Post (1608–69), the Mauritshuis in The Hague. In each case it is the Classical style of Palladio that has served as inspiration, rather than the more exuberant recent developments in Italy.

France saw the growth of a more individual Classical style, whose leading exponent was François Mansart (1598–1666). His secular buildings have high pitched roofs with even higher chimneys, and this vertical emphasis is countered by the rhythm of the windows on each storey and by the arrangement of simple geometrical volumes with Classical harmony. The Orders, though generally incorporated, are subordinated to the overall clarity of the design.

Banqueting House, Whitehall; *Inigo Jones, 1619–22.*
Jones's interior is very light and strongly sculptural, both in its use of a colonnade to support the balcony and in the plaster modelling around Rubens's painting (1635) on the panelled ceiling.

The main development of Baroque architecture took place in Rome, aided by the renewed vigour of papal and Church patronage. From the middle of the sixteenth century the city gave evidence of the urgent force of the Counter-Reformation: under successive popes ancient monuments were converted to ecclesiastical use, churches were built for the new aggressive Orders and work again went ahead on the completion of St Peter's. Giacomo della Porta (*c.* 1537–1602) had completed the dome by 1600, and then at last the decision was reached

to give the basilica the form of a Latin cross. The work of completion was entrusted to Carlo Maderna (1556–1629), whose nave was completed in 1626. Although faithful to Michelangelo in style, the additional length ruined the carefully planned view of the dome from the square in front of the church. In 1624 the young sculptor and architect Gian Lorenzo Bernini (1598–1680) was commissioned to construct a canopy over the high altar in St Peter's, and the elaborate *baldacchino,* supported on four twisting columns and topped by four large angels,

became the dynamic focal point of the interior of the basilica beneath the high dome (*see* p. 59). Later, after an unsuccessful attempt to build a belfry on the main façade, Bernini also brought back a sense of proportion to the exterior, building a massive colonnade around an oval piazza in front of the church. It is a gigantic portico 'to receive the faithful maternally with open arms'.

The works of Bernini and his contemporaries, which form the triumphs of Roman Baroque architecture, are a milestone in the history of the Renaissance style. The ideal of harmony and equilibrium is replaced by the striving for theatrical effect, and all the means at the architects' disposal were directed to this end. Michelangelo and Palladio had already shown the way with their sense of the siting of buildings and their manipulations of the effects of light and shade, but the Baroque architects strained to the utmost—without destroying—the style based on the Classical Orders and geometrical plans. They preferred the oval to the circle or square as the basis for many buildings and made much of the play of convex and concave curves set off against one another. In the interiors especially extensive use was made of false perspectives, of *trompe-l'oeil* (cheat the eye) painting and of dramatic lighting, so that whereas in Bramante's buildings the interior space and the architectural shell enclosing it are in harmonious equilibrium, in the great Baroque buildings the space seems to expand beyond the confining walls, which are themselves always in movement.

All these characteristics can be seen in the work of the three greatest Roman Baroque architects, Bernini, his pupil and rival Francesco Borromini (1599–1667), who was a nephew of Carlo Maderna, and the Florentine Pietro da Cortona (1596–1669), who was both painter and architect. As can be seen from his colonnade of St Peter's, Bernini excelled on the grandest scale, and his design for the Piazza Navona, which was on the site of the ancient Stadium of Domitian and therefore very long and narrow, is a masterpiece of planning, the fountains with their swirling sculptures integrating the length and connecting it to the dominant architectural feature of the piazza, Borromini's façade and towers for the church of S. Agnese. But Bernini could be equally successful on a small scale, as in his own favourite S. Andrea al Quirinale, designed on an oval plan.

Pietro da Cortona was a master of façades, and his church of S. Maria della Pace, Rome, matching his own design for the surrounding piazza, shows a rich use of contrasted curves, though the detail remains restrained. Borromini, who was the most unconventional of the three, had complete command of the articulation of space, even working in a very restricted area. The interiors of his two finest churches in Rome, S. Carlo alle Quattro Fontane and S. Ivo alla Sapienza, show extraordinary control of light and space, the one culminating in an oval dome, the other built up on the form of two interpenetrating triangles. On the outside S. Ivo is built at the end of a narrow court, the loggias of which the architect has skilfully integrated with the façade of the church, leading the eye on up to the fantastically constructed and decorated dome and lantern with a spiral top. Borromini's work has sometimes been seen as one of the most extreme forms of Baroque architecture, and it is true that his restless opposition of curves was an important influence on the exuberant Rococo of southern Germany and Austria, but his works are constructed with great rigour, and the complexities of his interior spaces are derived from the simplest geometrical elements. He reveals the essence of Baroque, which is not its waywardness, but—as in a Bach fugue—the extraordinary richness of both decoration and texture obtainable within an extremely rigid formal structure.

ABOVE **Piazza Navona, Rome**; *mid-17th century.* The replanning of Piazza Navona demonstrates the Baroque fusion of sculpture, architecture and nature in space. Borromini's concave façade to S. Agnese (begun 1653) faces the centrepiece of the whole composition, Bernini's Fountain of the Rivers (1648–51), whose twisting figures draw in the eye from every point in the square, to focus upon the antique obelisk.

RIGHT **S. Andrea al Quirinale, Rome**; *Bernini, 1658–70.* A late work, S. Andrea is based entirely on an oval plan. The unified conception of the church, the half oval of the wings beside the porch echoing the oval interior, concentrates all attention on the performance of the religious mysteries at the high altar.

S. Ivo alla Sapienza, Rome; *Borromini, begun 1642.*
The drawing shows the triangular planning of the church, which is related to the structural principles of Gothic architecture. The spiral lantern goes back to the traditions of the *ziggurat* (*cf.* the minaret at Samarra, p. 29).

Throughout the seventeenth century Rome remained the great centre of Baroque architecture, but Roman influence, often with characteristic regional variations, formed many local styles. In Sicily, Apulia and Naples beautiful churches and palaces were built, the last great monuments of Venice took shape—the most famous of these being the Salute church by Baldassare Longhena (1598–1682), with its dome seemingly held up by elaborate scrolls—but the lessons of Borromini were best learnt in Turin, capital of the Duchy of Piedmont, by Guarino Guarini (1624–83) and his followers. Guarini's buildings are among the most dramatic creations of the Baroque, his manipulation of light and space is unsurpassed, but most of all he demonstrates the Baroque architect's fascination with structure. In no way did the seventeenth century look forward to the nineteenth and twentieth centuries so much as in the daring innovations in constructional technique developed by architects, who loved to show off some seemingly impossible feat. Guarini's dome for the Chapel of the Holy Shroud in Turin (see p. 13) is the most sensational example, like a radiant ladder up to the Heavens, the masterpiece of an architect who had previously been a teacher of mathematics and philosophy.

OPPOSITE **Dome of Salute church, Venice;** *B. Longhena, 1630–87.* Longhena was one of a number of stage-designer architects in the Baroque period, an ' he took full advantage of the dramatic possibilities offered by this site on the entrance to the Grand Canal. The rich sculptural decoration is typically Venetian.

RIGHT **Dome of Chapel of Les Invalides, Paris;** *J. Hardouin Mansart, 1706.* The height of the dome occupies half the height of the church and the rest of the building is dominated by its fine proportions; whereas in Wren's St Paul's (begun 1675) and other domed churches of this period the dome is only one element in the monumental structure.

OPPOSITE **Painted ceiling, S. Ignazio, Rome;** *A. Pozzo, 1691–4.* This is the most successful of all the attempts to open out the space of a church or hall with painting in false perspective, without any use of stucco. There is only one point (about one third of the way down the nave) from which the full effect can be seen, and looking back from near the high altar all the false architecture falls completely flat.

The illusions of space and light, which were such an integral part of Baroque interiors, were difficult to create in the long nave of a church or in a great hall, and here painting was often called into service as part of the architecture. In particular, a technique of illusionism was perfected, which employed false perspective to extend walls and ceilings far beyond their actual positions. This technique had already been used by Giulio Romano in the Hall of the Giants in his Palazzo del Té, but its most extreme applications date from the last quarter of the seventeenth century. In Rome two churches were decorated with ceilings that are triumphs of the *trompel'oeil* technique: the Gesù, painted by Baciccia (1639–1709), and S. Ignazio, painted by Andrea del Pozzo (1642–1709). Both show the Heavens opening above the church, and by a combination of false architecture and figure painting create an ambiguity which also allows the inhabitants of Heaven to come down and hover on their clouds within the church.

By 1700 Roman influence had spread throughout the western world, and there were already a great number of buildings in European styles on the American continent. The settlers in North America, many of them refugees from religious intolerance, built simple dwellings, meeting houses and churches, but in Spanish and Portuguese America the militant new Orders of the Roman Catholic church had been active since the mid-sixteenth century, and dozens of churches and monasteries were built even in small settlements in Peru, Ecuador, Guatemala, Mexico and Brazil. They adapted Spanish Mannerism to the local materials, generally working in styles many decades out of date in Europe and making extensive use of crude but lively carvings, which often—in the Spanish manner—cover every available surface.

In France the architecture of Louis XIV's court had to be on the grandest possible scale, and France's rivalry of Spain and of papal power in Rome had to be expressed in architectural terms. Paris must outshine Rome and the king had to have a palace that would eclipse the

Escorial. The most obvious landmark for emulation in Rome was the dome of St Peter's, and the French particularly devoted themselves to the problem (not solved in St Peter's) of raising a dome high enough to harmonize with the façade of the church. The most accomplished of the seventeenth-century domed churches of Paris— surpassed only by Christopher Wren's St Paul's Cathedral in London, which was based on French models— was that of Les Invalides, the royal hospital, built by Jules Hardouin Mansart (1646–1708). His handling of the Orders and of Renaissance decoration shows French clarity and restraint, and the fine effect of the dome is attributable partly to the central plan of the church and partly to the device of covering the real masonry dome with a false one of timber to increase its height.

RIGHT **Dome of S. Lorenzo, Turin;** *Guarini, begun 1668.* S. Lorenzo is planned as an octagon with concave sides set in a square; the construction of the dome echoes this, using eight binding arches (similar to Moorish domes of the 10th century) to form an octagon that supports the circular lantern. Guarini's superb control of light as an element of the architecture and the clarity of his geometry (note the pentagonal openings above the main windows) is matched only in his own dome for the Chapel of the Holy Shroud (*see* p. 13).

ABOVE **Gardens of Versailles;** *A. Le Nôtre, begun 1667.*
The sense of order on such a vast scale was achieved by a formal plan with its axis running through the centre of the palace and continuing, as seen here, across the Bassin de Latone and down the Grand Canal.

RIGHT **Royal Hospital, Greenwich;** *Wren and others, begun 1696.*
Wren had to incorporate Inigo Jones's Queen's House, which he made the focus of the long vista, using a low colonnade to lead the eye down from the domed corner blocks and so overcome the much smaller scale of Jones's building.

The plans for Louis XIV's palace began with the grandiose façade of the Louvre in Paris, owing much to the designs of Claude Perrault (1613–88) and carried out under the supervision of Louis le Vau (1612–70), but more majestic still was the enlargement of Versailles. Le Vau had already worked with the garden designer André Le Nôtre (1613–1700) at the magnificent château of Vaux-le-Vicomte, but at Versailles with, later, the help of Jules Hardouin Mansart, they produced a monument that remained unsurpassed in its scale and which has become a symbol of the age of absolute monarchy. The designs were not for buildings alone, but for the complex taken as a whole, and the elaborate garden was of great importance—as frequently in Baroque architecture. Architects' plans showed an increasing awareness of the relation of buildings to their surroundings, and the piazza, the planned town, and the villa or country house in its landscape setting are all examples of this development. But the park had a symbolic as well as an aesthetic significance: it represented the success of humans in creating order out of chaos in harmony with nature. More still than the ostentatious state rooms of the palace, Le Nôtre's gardens of Versailles are Baroque architecture on the grandest scale.

In England too the restoration of the monarchy had resulted in new royal buildings and a general revival of architectural activity. The outstanding architect was Sir Christopher Wren (1632–1723), whose work, following in the classical tradition of Inigo Jones, established a fully independent English Renaissance style. Like Guarini, Wren was a mathematician, and his greatest achievement, St Paul's Cathedral, shows a comparable technical mastery, but in a more sober untheatrical vein. It harks back to the harmonious ideals of the early Renaissance in Italy with its simple equilibrium of space, though on a far larger scale. St Paul's became the focal point of Wren's plan to rebuild London after the Great Fire of 1666 and it was set off by a forest of spired churches in the City. As has often been pointed out, Wren's spires are a direct continuation of the native Gothic tradition of spired churches, but carried out in Renaissance forms and certainly showing the influence of Borromini. The same is true of his work in the universities of Oxford and Cambridge and his extensions to the royal palace of Hampton Court. His finest secular achievement was the Royal Hospital at Greenwich, built between Inigo Jones's Queen's House and the river Thames. This is a palace of Baroque monumentality, making effective use of long colonnades of paired columns, integrated with the whole complex by two majestic domed towers.

Sir John Vanbrugh (1664–1726) and Nicholas Hawksmoor (1661–1736) worked with Wren at Greenwich and they were his two most important followers. Hawksmoor, whose City churches in London were less Classical than Wren's, sometimes with quite bizarre designs, collaborated with Vanbrugh on his two most ambitious projects, both among the grandest of English country houses. Blenheim Palace was built as a gift from the nation to the victorious Duke of Marlborough, with an elaborate landscape garden—order imposed on nature—by Lancelot 'Capability' Brown (1716–83), and just as magnificent is Castle Howard in Yorkshire, whose exaggerations of scale proclaim it a work fully in the Baroque tradition, while it retains its specifically English character.

The religious battles of the seventeenth century raged most bloodily in Germany and for the period of the Thirty Years War (1618–48) more fine buildings were destroyed than erected. Nor did things ease everywhere with the peace. Austria, the heartland of the Empire, was under pressure from the Turks and in 1683 Vienna came under siege. The defeat of the Turks at the Battle

of Kahlenberg effectively removed this menace and was the signal for the start of a great spate of building. In Vienna itself the noble families built new town houses and also summer palaces in the areas outside the city walls which had been devastated by the Turks. Two architects stand out from the rest, each of whom had studied in Rome under Carlo Fontana (1634–1714), the assistant of both Bernini and Pietro da Cortona. Johann Bernhard Fischer von Erlach (1656–1723), the court architect, worked very much in the grand Roman manner, more so than the younger Lukas von Hildebrandt (1668–1745), a military engineer who was patronized by the great general Prince Eugen of Savoy, and had accompanied him on his campaigns in northern Italy. Fischer von Erlach was a prolific architect and undertook many churches (the celebrated Karlskirche is his masterpiece), monuments, summer palaces and town palaces in Vienna. Viennese town palaces generally fronted on narrow streets, and although the façades were sometimes quite elaborate, there was hardly room to appreciate them, and the grand entrance was made inside the house in the great staircase (*Treppenhaus*). Prince Eugen's palace by Fischer von Erlach shows how expertly he could create a magnificent effect in an enclosed space, using figures of giant captives to support the staircase.

Garden front, Castle Howard; *Vanbrugh, 1701–14.*
Vanbrugh had the most vivid dramatic imagination of the English Baroque architects, and this sense of theatre enabled him to create strongly picturesque effects on a massive scale. He had the amateur architect's advantage of having made the Grand Tour and seen the latest foreign architecture at first hand, so that buildings such as Castle Howard, with its long façades and central dome, are related more closely to the common European tradition than those of most of his English contemporaries.

Staircase (Treppenhaus) of Prince Eugen's town palace, Vienna; *J. B. Fischer von Erlach, 1696.*
By incorporating sculpture into his architecture— using figures that have nothing in common with the serene caryatids of ancient Greece—Fischer von Erlach has heightened the dramatic effect of the great Baroque entrance staircase.

71

LEFT **Upper Belvedere, Vienna**; *L. von Hildebrandt, 1721–2.* The ideal of monumentality is here replaced by one of elegance, with balanced volumes and fine surface decoration. The taste for the exotic and picturesque was certainly stimulated by the publication, also in 1721, of Fischer von Erlach's *Outline for an Historical Architecture*, the first treatise to include discussion of Egyptian and Chinese architecture.
OPPOSITE **High altar, Weltenburg**; *C. D. and E. Q. Asam, 1721.* The uninhibited work of the Asams shows their debt to Bernini and the obviously sculptural qualities of Roman Baroque. The church at Weltenburg was built by Cosmas Damian Asam, while the theatrical altar is the work of his brother.

St Nicholas, Malá Strana, Prague; *Christoph Dientzenhofer, 1703–11.* The strongly curved bays of the nave and the controlled handling of light are both evidence of the influence of Guarini, who had built a church near Prague. The dome and bell-tower of the church were comp'eted (*c.* 1750) by Christoph's son Kilian Ignaz Dientzenhofer, who studied with his father and with Hildebrandt. The influence of Guarini, and through him of Borromini —both their constructions of space and light and their fluttering decoration —came to the lands of southern Germany and the Austrian Empire through such architects as Hildebrandt and the Dientzenhofers.

Hildebrandt's greatest work for Eugen was his summer palace, the Belvedere, which consists of two palace buildings on a rising hill, divided by a long garden with lawns, pools and fountains. The upper palace is a wonderfully original building, with a wide triple porch, octagonal domed pavilions at the ends of the façade and an exotic roof, that has been compared to the military tents of the vanquished Turks, but seems closer to Chinese architecture. The Belvedere demonstrates the new turn given to the Baroque style in southern Germany and Austria; the emphasis is more on decoration than construction, and there is an attempt to give an appearance of weightlessness to the exteriors of the buildings and an airy lightness to the interiors.

The years after 1700 saw a quite extraordinary amount of building in this area, much ecclesiastical and much of that monastic. Of all the great monasteries the most dramatically sited is the abbey of Melk by Jakob Prandtauer (1660–1726), but everywhere schools and families of architects were at work with their teams of painters,

stuccoists and decorators and, although their work was uneven, the best is architecture at its most joyous and its most theatrical. Indeed many elements seem (like the boxes overlooking each side of the choir) to have been actually taken over from theatre design, while windows were arranged to spotlight the sculpture.

In Prague the Dientzenhofer family undertook many commissions and had a better understanding than most of the architectural handling of space, so that their work depends less on sheer exuberance of decoration. The church of St Nicholas in Malá Strana, Prague, shows all the devices of Baroque architecture, the dramatic lighting, the *trompe-l'oeil* decoration, the florid stucco work and lively sculpture, but the attention is held by the architecture itself, with the undulating balustrade running from the organ loft over each curved bay, light streaming in from above it.

In the work of the brothers Asam, who were active in and around Munich in the first third of the eighteenth century, the theatrical dominates the purely architectural, and their high altar at Weltenburg, with sculpture showing St George rescuing the princess from the dragon, is dramatically back-lit by concealed windows. They too had studied under Fontana in Rome, and their work remains in the mainstream of Baroque architecture, though of an unsophisticated kind.

The same peasant quality is found in the work of many of their contemporaries, though for the most part they abandoned the dramatic gestures of the Baroque and adopted the more decorative Rococo style. The most prolific of all the south German Rococo architects was Johann Michael Fischer (*c.* 1691–1766), whose finest work is the church at Ottobeuren, but the masterpiece of the style is the little pilgrimage church of Die Wies in the Bavarian Alps by Dominikus Zimmermann (1685–1766). The main body of the church is based on an oval plan and is well lit, giving an overall feeling of spaciousness and brightness, while the decorative scheme, in white and gold stucco with a *trompe-l'oeil* ceiling in pale colours, contributes to this effect and is never overpowering. The Italian origins of this style can be pointed to in many features, but the works of Zimmermann and J. M. Fischer helped to establish a new local tradition, which dominated the architecture of this region for nearly a century.

Choir of church of Die Wies; *D. Zimmermann, 1744–54.*
Here the emphasis is on an open space, on overall brightness, on lively colours and on restless, asymmetrical decorative forms, based on leaves and plants, shells, curtains and pelmets, etc.

RIGHT **S. Giorgio, Ragusa, Sicily;**
R. Gagliardi, begun 1746.
Sicilian churches had traditionally incorporated the bell-tower in the façade, and Gagliardi's translation of this into full-scale Baroque is brilliant. Elements that contribute to the effect are the broad flight of steps, the exotically carved door, the curved façade, the triple columns stepped forward, the swirling volutes surmounted by statues of saints.

BELOW **Garden front, Stupinigi Palace;**
F. Juvarra, begun 1729.
Like the architects of the north, Juvarra is here more concerned with the relationship of volumes than with sculptural effects. The focus of the building is the central hall, with wings set off at an angle from the main axis of the building.

In Italy too, much of the most vigorous architecture was to be found outside the main centres, for Carlo Fontana, though an influential teacher, exercised a dead hand on architecture in Rome. Sicily had a flourishing school of architects in the eighteenth century, who built villas and town palaces for the nobility and many large churches. There had always been a stronger emphasis on surface decoration in Sicily (as also in Apulia, where an individual style was maintained throughout the century), but in the work of the greatest of the Sicilian school, Rosario Gagliardi (active 1721–70), structural elements are handled in a fully architectural way. His cathedral of S. Giorgio at Ragusa, situated dramatically at the top of flights of steps, has a convex belfry tower built in three tiers forming the façade, and Gagliardi's handling of the columns, the elaborate pediments, the stepping back and forward of the planes and the integration of the sculptural, decorative and architectural elements is masterly.

In Turin it was the Sicilian Filippo Juvarra (1678–1736), another pupil of Fontana and the last in the line of great Italian Baroque architects, who undertook the rebuilding of the royal palace (working with the Rococo decorator and furniture-designer Pietro Piffetti) and who designed a massive 'hunting lodge' at Stupinigi, one of the many buildings throughout Europe that took the vast scale of Versailles as its model. The list of Juvarra's other buildings is enormous and includes sketches, never

carried out, for a new royal palace in Lisbon, commissioned by King João V, whose reign saw the second flowering of Portuguese architecture. The exploitation of the newly discovered gold-mines of Brazil meant that Portuguese architects could carry out work of incredible richness. Lavish gilding was used over elaborately carved wood, sometimes in conjunction with precious woods, also imported from America, or combined with traditional pictorial tiles. There are beautiful churches with golden interiors in Oporto and other northern towns, and many examples too in Brazil itself. Another feature of Portuguese Baroque (also exported to Brazil, where one half-Indian architect and sculptor, known as O Aleijadinho, 'the little dwarf', carried out some outstanding work as late as the years around 1800) was the grand façade flanked by two bell towers, with the decorative elements carved in dark granite against whitewashed walls. These are ornate frontispieces with little structural ingenuity in the common European Baroque tradition, but occasionally, when they are approached by many tiered staircases, as at Lamego or the pilgrimage church of Bom Jesus near Braga, they can become the focus of a magnificently dramatic vista.

The Portuguese were in part indebted to contemporary developments in Spain. The use of overall surface decoration had been a characteristic of Spanish architecture since Islamic times, and around 1700 it again became the most important element in the local Baroque

style, seen at its best in the work of Francisco Hurtado (1669–1725) and his followers in the Cartuja of Granada. The architectural elements remained fairly simple, but were overwhelmed with a restless decoration of cornices, which did everything to contradict expected structural functions. Even later, the Obradoiro (work of gold) façade built on to the ancient pilgrimage church of Santiago de Compostela by Fernando de Casas y Nóvoa (d. *c.* 1751) is essentially a decorative frontispiece, but on the grandest scale, with a marvellous structural harmony between the central triumphal arch

RIGHT **S. Francisco Acatepec, near Puebla;** *second half 18th century.* The rich overall decoration and the use of glazed tiles both derived from Spain, but were treated with even greater extravagance by Mexican architects. Here as well as tiles there are large ceramic columns on the characteristic three-storey façade.

BELOW **Trasparente chapel, Toledo Cathedral;** *N. Tomé, 1732.* The illusionistic effect was created by cutting away part of the roof and building up a tall dormer with a window that sheds bright light on the altar, but is invisible to the spectator; for on looking through the opening he sees, beyond the crowd of angels, a fresco of Christ enthroned in Heaven.

approached by an earlier (1605) double staircase, the massive square bell towers and the solid blocks of the wings on either side.

The most remarkable of all Spanish Baroque works is the theatrical *Trasparente* in the otherwise Gothic cathedral of Toledo by Narciso Tomé (active 1715–42). This is in fact an illusionistic altar of the Blessed Sacrament, with rich sculpture, lit from above by a concealed window, which is surrounded by frescoed walls that seem to afford a glimpse of Heaven through an opening manned by cherubim. The *Trasparente* epitomizes the drama of Baroque and emphasizes the contributions of paintings and sculpture—and light—as architectural elements.

Spanish styles too were exported to America and, in Mexico particularly, were recreated with yet more fantasy. Buildings such as the Santuario de Ocotlán or the tiled S. Francisco Acatepec, near Puebla, show great originality in their decoration and in the materials used, and are characteristic of the Mexican delight in elaborate and, literally, colourful architecture.

The second half of the eighteenth century saw the triumph of Rococo in secular buildings throughout southern Europe. This highly decorative style originated in France and, although in Germany it was often used with real architectural effect, the French used it more as a feature of interior decoration than of architectural structures. This is not to deny the beauty and extreme refinement of some of the French Rococo interiors, particularly the works of Robert de Cotte (1656–1735) and Gabriel-Germain Boffrand (1667–1754). Their influence was also widespread in Germany, and can be seen in the sumptuous decoration of the state rooms in the prince-archbishop's palace (*Residenz*) at Würzburg, where varieties of coloured marble, stucco and frescoes are all used. De Cotte himself prepared plans for the palace at Würzburg, but they were rejected and the building that was erected followed the plans of Balthasar Neumann (1687–1753). Neumann was the greatest master of spatial complications among the south German architects, and his pilgrimage church of Vierzehnheiligen is built on a plan of intersecting ovals, centred round the altar, which is designed more like the top of a ceremonial carriage. At Würzburg Neumann's finest achievement is the great staircase—a feature that architects since Michelangelo and Palladio had used with increasingly dramatic effect—which leads up from the low entrance-hall to the main floor through a spacious open area covered with a magnificent fresco by the greatest of all the Baroque ceiling painters, Giambattista Tiepolo (1697–1770).

Of equal richness is the Amalienburg hunting lodge of the Nymphenburg Palace at Munich, built by the Bavarian court architect François Cuvilliés (1695–1768) and decorated with stucco-work by J. B. Zimmermann (the brother of Dominikus). The centrepiece is a circular banqueting hall, where the architect used the device of mirrors set in the wall to add to the effect of insubstantiality. More extravagant still are the 'porcelain rooms' in the Royal Palace in Madrid and elsewhere, decorated with *chinoiseries,* which exemplify the taste throughout Europe for a touch of the exotic in Rococo decoration.

The Rococo reached as far as Russia, where western styles had become increasingly favoured since the reign of Peter the Great (1685–1725). At first Italian styles predominated, but the work of Bartolommeo Francesco Rastrelli (1700–71), a pupil of de Cotte, is almost wholly French, though with some traditional Russian elements, and his huge palaces in St Petersburg (Leningrad) show Rococo on a gigantic scale. Later still, English Palladianism flourished in Russia with the work of the Scotsman Charles Cameron (*c.* 1740–1812).

LEFT **Staircase, Würzburg Residenz;** *B. Neumann, 1737–50, painting 1753.* The aesthetic achievement here matches the brilliant technical feats: Neumann's in covering the great staircase hall with a single unsupported vault, Tiepolo's in frescoing this with a single composition.

BELOW **Amalienburg, Nymphenburg park;** *F. Cuvilliés, 1734–9.* The pale contrasting colours, the use of mirrors, the silvered and gilt stucco, are all derived from French Rococo models—in strong contrast to the Italianate work of the Asam brothers (*see* p.73).

Porcelain room, Royal Palace, Madrid; *c.1765.* The room was decorated with Spanish Buen Retiro porcelain by Neapolitan artists as part of the exotic decorations devised for King Charles III. A similar room had already been created in the King's summer palace at Aranjuez, and both are modelled on the porcelain room in the Neapolitan royal villa at Portici, where the local Capodimonte porcelain was used.

Exoticism, or at least the reliance on models from earlier or alien styles, became an increasingly significant feature of architecture in the course of the eighteenth century, as the possibilities of Baroque were exhausted —although it was generally the result of a pursuit of the picturesque rather than a revival or renewal in the revolutionary sense which characterized the later Neo-Classical and Gothic Revival movements. In England, Nicholas Hawksmoor was particularly inventive in his designs for London churches and went for inspiration for his spires to engravings of Classical antiquities. One church, St George's, Bloomsbury, which has a severe classical portico, is topped by a stepped pyramid (based on reconstructions of the Mausoleum of Halicarnassus)

surmounted by a statue of the patron saint; another of his most beautiful churches, Christ Church, Spitalfields, very effectively combines the idea of the Gothic spire with a Renaissance church. In Oxford, following the example of Wren, he used pure Gothic for his gateway to All Souls College and he also built the Gothic west towers of Westminster Abbey.

James Gibbs (1682–1754), who also built London churches and undertook work in the universities, was by contrast the one British architect who did interpret the legacy of Wren in a more consequential way, drawing also on his experience in Rome, where he too had been a pupil of Fontana. But his colleagues in Britain, although they looked to Italy, did not go to Fontana,

Bernini or Borromini for inspiration, still less to the Rococo style that had developed from their work in Austria, Germany and France. English architects looked back a century to Inigo Jones, a century more to Palladio and fifteen centuries more still to Antiquity. Their patrons, and many of the gentleman architects as well, spent a year or more on the Grand Tour, and the ultimate destination was Rome, having taken in Venice and Palladio's villas on the mainland on the way down. The leader of the Palladian movement was Lord Burlington (1694–1753), himself an amateur architect and the designer of his own Paladian villa at Chiswick; but the closest imitator of Palladio's work was the Scotsman Colen Campbell (d. 1729), whose Mereworth House is based very closely on Palladio's famous Villa Rotonda. This was also the model for Burlington's Chiswick and appeared in one or two other English guises around the same time. Palladianism also became extremely popular in Ireland, where the leading architect was the German Richard Castle (c. 1690–1751). Burlington's chief protégé was William Kent (1685–1748), who was both architect and landscape gardener and who created perhaps the most grandly Classical interior of the whole period in the Great Hall of Holkham Hall, which skilfully combines Antique models with the architect's (or his patron's) own imaginative ideas. Kent's garden designs also show a significant deviation from the theories of the Renaissance, in that the picturesque is allowed to dominate the ideal of order in nature, and among the picturesque elements are architectural pavilions and follies in a number of different styles, including Chinese, 'rustic' and Gothic.

Gothic was even on one occasion considered suitable for a whole house, Horace Walpole's Strawberry Hill. This is pure exoticism, but it is handled as effectively as the *chinoiseries* of Madrid and becomes a sort of Rococo–Gothic.

ABOVE **Entrance hall. Holkham Hall;**
W. Kent, begun 1734.
Both Kent and his patron Lord Burlington (who may well have had a hand in the designs for the house) had been on the Grand Tour—as too had Lord Leicester, for whom the house was built. The apsed hall is based on designs by Palladio and on Roman architecture; although derivative, it makes a very grand entrance to the house.

RIGHT **The Gallery, Strawberry Hill, Twickenham;**
Thomas Pitt, 1759–62.
The Gothic decoration of Horace Walpole's house was undertaken by various amateur architects under the general guidance of Walpole himself and his builder William Robinson. The 'Gothick' of the gallery, with its rich ceiling (based on an aisle of Henry VII's Chapel in Westminster Abbey), canopies, and mirrors covered with fine tracery, is—like *chinoiserie*—an exotic form of Rococo decoration.

RIGHT **Royal Crescent, Bath**; *J. Wood the younger, 1767–75.*
The uniformity of the great sweep of the building was to be ensured by having all the doors painted white, while, for convenience, the house walls between the Ionic columns are not curved. In spite of the fine urban developments there, Bath in early Victorian times was to have some of the worst slums in Britain.

LEFT **Shirley Plantation, Virginia**; *1723–70.*
Virginia has some of the finest Colonial architecture, notably the Governor's House at Williamsburg and the tobacco planters' houses; Shirley, on the James River, is among the earliest of these. Its most notable feature is the great wooden portico, a Palladian element adapted to the local climate and materials.

FAR LEFT **Petit Trianon**; *A. J. Gabriel, 1761–8.*
Unlike Palladianism, French Classicism was neither imitation nor revival, but simply a pure and harmonious use of the Classical idiom.

LEFT **Longfellow House, Cambridge, Mass.**; *1759.*
A fine mansion that shows English Palladianism fitted to American conditions. The use of weatherproof clapboarding had been common since the 17th century, and remained popular in America. The style resembles that of Peter Harrison (1716–75), the leading architect of the age, whose King's Chapel, Boston, shows Gibbs's influence.

RIGHT **Detail of house front, Mount Pleasant, Philadelphia**; *1761.*
The style is derived from stone buildings, but here rubble walls are covered with stucco scored in imitation of dressed stone, the corner stones (quoins) are replaced with red brickwork, and the roof balustrade is of wood.

Examples of the picturesque are to be found throughout Europe in the late eighteenth century, but in France the purity of English Palladianism was matched by a still greater refinement of the existing tendencies towards Classicism and simplicity. Nowhere was this carried out with greater success than in the Petit Trianon at Versailles by Ange-Jacques Gabriel (1698–1782), although its style makes no overt reference to Antiquity.

Classical influence was demonstrated in an entirely different way in England in the planning of new districts in the towns, which were beginning to undergo the growth that would lead to the urban horrors of the mid-nineteenth century. The Bath architect family of the Woods conceived the idea of adapting the ancient Roman circus or half-circus to the planning of streets, and from these originate the ubiquitous crescents and circuses of Georgian town-plans. The houses themselves were in a plain Renaissance style, often incorporating a colonnade or pilasters covering the top two floors, while the lower floor might be rusticated, and sometimes the monotony of a block which made up the side of a square, a terrace or a crescent, would be broken up by the addition of a central pediment or by differentiated end pavilions.

In the American colonies, though there were no truly monumental buildings, local architects took the styles derived from Wren, Gibbs and the Palladians and produced their own characteristic versions. In the northern states much use was made of clapboard, and a fine example of a small house built with great simplicity but showing a good understanding of harmonious proportions is the historic Longfellow House in Cambridge, Mass., which was George Washington's headquarters in 1775. In the south a local development was the enlargement of the entrance portico into the dominant feature of the main façade, often providing a loggia—as the climate demanded—on lower and upper floors, running nearly the full length of the façade. This feature was transferred to ecclesiastical architecture as well.

Between 1450 and 1750 the map of the world had changed and it was possible not only for Englishmen—and Americans—to go on the Grand Tour, but Europeans had colonized India, much of Africa and southeast Asia and had established vigorous trading links with China. Already exotic styles had been absorbed into European architecture, and we must now go back in time to see what had been the origins of the styles which the western travellers found and marvelled at.

CHAPTER 6

THE CIVILIZATIONS OF THE EAST

OPPOSITE **Central stupa of Borobodur;**
9th century AD.
The focal point of one of the greatest architectural monuments of Buddhism, the main *stupa* is of an austere simplicity with almost no decoration other than the stylized lotus base —although the lower square terraces of the temple contain narrative sculpture of the highest quality. The Bodhisattva figure is from one of the smaller *stupas* left unrestored, and was originally enclosed by latticed stonework, like that visible on the two higher platforms; note how the patterning of the stonework is varied on the different stages.

It is necessary to go back nearly two thousand years to trace the beginnings of the eastern architectural tradition. Again it is the religious architecture which is paramount, but it is essential to discard western conceptions in order to understand its intention and significance. To start with, Buddhism, the most important of the eastern religions, is not a congregational religion, and the earliest shrines were places of pilgrimage, not focal points of community or city life, as were churches and mosques in the west. The shrine was the goal of a journey, but was also a part of it in that the pilgrim would approach it and walk round it in his effort to attain to virtue. It is therefore essentially architecture to be moved through, or even, if the roles are reversed and it is seen from the point of view of the spectator, it is 'dynamic' rather than static architecture. In addition, the symbolic significance, particularly of the plan of a site, was both more pronounced and more explicit than in the west, a cosmic meaning being given to the square site and the progression towards the central feature. Nor was there an exclusivity of religion in the sense of Christianity or Islam, and in India—which is the starting point for eastern religious architecture—Hinduism and Buddhism developed side by side for a thousand years as different aspects of the same culture.

The focus of the Buddhist shrine is the *stupa,* which generally takes the form of a mound covering or enclosing relics of the Buddha. Nearby, and aligned with the *stupa,* will generally be a *vihara,* or monastery for monks who tend the shrine. Among the earliest *stupas* were those erected in the third century BC by King Ashoka, who was largely responsible for the introduction and spread of Buddhism, but among the oldest ones to survive—and heavily restored at that—are the three *stupas* at Sanchi. They are not enclosed within any building, and the approach to each is interrupted only by gates, or archways, which hold the attention of the pilgrim on his way to perform the circumambulation (*pradakshina*) of the *stupa* itself. By the gates and balustrades defining the shrine the surrounding landscape is made to serve as architecture. This is brought about in a very different way in the caves of Ajanta, where each *stupa* is enclosed within a preaching hall, or *chaitya,* cut from the living rock. Almost invariably a Buddhist site is made up of a complex of shrines, and at Ajanta there are twenty-nine caves, both monasteries and shrines, some of them decorated with superb wall-paintings that still survive. The earliest caves date from the first two centuries BC, but the main groups were built *c.* AD 450–650. The *stupa* is positioned in an apse at the far end of the cave, which is generally entered through an elaborate porch, and is approached by a colonnade which leads round the shrine. The technique of rock-cutting and the forms, which imitate wooden architecture, are derived ultimately from Persia, after the defeat and dispersal of the Persians by Alexander the Great.

RIGHT **Thuparama, Anuradhapura;** *3rd century* BC, *reconstructed c.* AD *1200.* Ceylon contains some of the most ancient and holy Buddhist shrines. The Thuparama shows the traditional *stupa* form (known as a *dagoba* in Ceylon) surrounded by terraces, with nearby the *vihara* of the monks, of which only the pillars that supported the upper floor survive.

BELOW **Great stupa, Sanchi;** *3rd–2nd centuries* BC, *restored.* This is—in form at least— the earliest surviving *stupa* in India, and is remarkable for its finely carved gates and simple balustrades.

The most monumental Buddhist *stupa* is not to be found in India, but was built, after Indian conquests, at Borobodur in Java. Here, the central *stupa* is at the top of nine terraces surrounded by many little *stupas,* some with openwork carving to half-reveal a statue of a Bodhisattva. Again this architecture must be thought of as slowly revolving as the pilgrim approaches the shrine; he glimpses the main *stupa* through archways, but his vision is constantly interrupted as the narrative carvings on the terraces are resumed and hold his attention, or smaller *stupas* block the view.

The Hindu temple is similarly dynamic architecture. It is generally made up of a square central shrine topped by a pyramidal tower (derived from the *stupa*) with other halls attached on the same axis, to form a long rectangular complex, approached through one or a series of elaborate towered gates. It was rare for a temple to be completed according to a unified plan, and even the halls added to the main shrine were sometimes given quite separate treatment, so that many Hindu temples were built up over a considerable period of time, with

RIGHT **Chaitya XIX, Ajanta**; *c. AD 550*.
Both the technique of rock-cut architecture and the form of the pillared hall are of Persian origin, although the style of the work is by now wholly Indian. The interior and the porch of *chaitya* XIX are among the most richly decorated and finely proportioned of the Ajanta caves.

even less sense of stylistic unity than was the case with the medieval European cathedrals. The earliest Hindu temples date from the fifth century AD, but the customary plan was evolved a century or two later by the Pallavan dynasty in south India. One of its most important early appearances in the north is in the Kailasanatha Temple at Ellora, near Ajanta and the site of a number of rock-cut temples. An even greater virtuosity of rock-carving is shown here, with the temple not in a cave but carved in the round out of the mountain and decorated in the most elaborate way.

Far greater elaboration still can be seen in the Orissan temples in north-east India, where the greatest surviving complex is at Bhubaneshwar. This is dominated by the Lingaraja temple, where the pyramidal tower over the shrine has been raised to a height of over one hundred and eighty feet and has the most fanciful deep-cut carving—undertaken after the building had been erected, as if in fact it had been cut from the rock like the earlier buildings. Much of the decoration is also derived from earlier structures of wood or of reeds.

ABOVE **Detail of Kailasanatha temple, Ellora**; *c. AD 760*.
Cut from the living rock, the Kailasa offers the most extraordinary richness of sculptural decoration and architectural form. The massive pyramidal roof is a characteristic feature of Indian temple architecture. The temple was dedicated to the god Shiva.

RIGHT **Lingaraja temple, Bhubaneshwar**; AD *1000*.
The greatest monument of the Orissan style, the tower is decorated with a pattern of repeated eaves and small superimposed towers, all carved after the masonry was in position. The interior, approached through the other temple buildings, occupies less than half the width of the tower.

The temples at Khajuraho in central north India also survived the widespread destruction undertaken by the puritan Moslem conquerors, and these are particularly remarkable for their sculptural decoration, much of it showing erotic scenes. The most impressive surviving temples in southern India date from a later period, the time of the Nayaka dynasty, who after defeating the Moslems in the seventeenth century re-established the centre of Hindu culture in the south of the peninsula. Two of the later temples, at Madura and Sriringam, are quite outstanding. The growth of the buildings at Sriringam shows the way in which a temple complex developed. The shrine is surrounded by a square precinct, with, on the axis of the shrine, a great gate tower, or *gopura*. As the temple was enlarged a succession of walls was built, each outside and surrounding the last, and (as with the succession of pylons in an Egyptian temple) each *gopura* had to outdo its predecessor, so that the approach to the shrine from the outside leads through a succession of gates, which decrease in size as the shrine is approached, while this itself is architecturally comparatively insignificant. This apparent anti-climax is nevertheless a remarkably effective approach to the holy place, as long as it is made without the preconception of what a dramatic approach should be.

A contrast to this method of gradually building up an architectural complex is found in an earlier temple, not on Indian soil, though within the Indian tradition, at Angkor Wat in Cambodia. Built originally as a funerary temple for the deified king of the Khmers, Suryavarman II, in the twelfth century, Angkor Wat is

LEFT **Two gopurams, Vishnu temple, Sriringam;** *17th century.* The temple is contained within seven rectangular enclosures, broken by a succession of *gopurams* (gate towers) on each central axis, twenty-one in all, descending in size as they approach the central shrine; the two outermost *gopurams* on the east side are shown here.

RIGHT **Shwe Dagon temple, Rangoon;** *18th century.* The traditional form of the *stupa* is enriched by the lavish gilding, and is set off by the surrounding shrines built in the ornate traditional Burmese style of wooden architecture.

LEFT **Lakshmana temple, Khajuraho;** *950–1050.* This gives a clear view of the strongly emphasized axis of the temple, leading from the flight of steps, flanked by corner shrines, through a number of halls with their pyramidal roofs to the tall *shikara* tower. The rich and varied decoration—including the superb erotic sculptures—does not obscure the basic form of the building.

constructed according to a consistent plan and is on a vast scale. It exemplifies the cosmic significance of the Hindu royal temple: the central tower represents the sacred mountain as the axis of the world, enshrining the essence of kingship, the moats are the oceans and the outer walls the mountains which surround the earth.

Angkor is only one of many monuments in neighbouring countries, which are ultimately derived from Indian architecture. Buddhist shrines and monasteries were built in individual local styles in Nepal and Tibet to the north, and east across the Bay of Bengal in Burma. One of the finest temple complexes is the Shwe Dagon, which dominates the city of Rangoon, in its present form no earlier than the eighteenth century, but going back hundreds of years further in tradition. The form is still the circular mound around which the pilgrim performs his *pradakshina*, but its rich gilding and decoration make it one of the most sumptuous buildings in the east, and in spite of its very obvious Indian derivation it is in a form and style characteristically Burmese.

India has been the watershed of the two surviving world civilizations. It has been subject to influences from the west, from Persia and through Afghanistan, after the conquests of Alexander the Great and after the Moslem invasions, though in each case the influences were absorbed and transformed in characteristically Indian ways; through conquest it gave rise to local schools of architecture further east in the Indian tradition, which sometimes even surpassed their model; and by the spread of Buddhism it strongly influenced the forms of Chinese architecture and its derivatives.

Temple of Angkor Wat;
12th century.
The symmetrical rectangular plan of the building is reflected in all the outer enclosures, and also in the relationship of the temple complex to the Khmer city of Angkor Thom, with which all roads are aligned in a completely regular way.

ABOVE **Inner shrine, Izume Taisha;** *3rd century* AD *, reconstructed 1744.*
The shrine shows the traditional Japanese style current before the advent of Buddhism, with the tremendous variety of treatment given to wooden elements.

TOP RIGHT **The Great Wall of China;**
3rd century BC *and later.*

BELOW RIGHT **Ch'i-yin pagoda with thirteen eaves, White Horse temple, Lo-yang;**
8th century AD.
The characteristic T'ang pagoda was built on a square plan, of brick or masonry, with a number of projecting eaves; often, as here, a gracefully curved profile was given to the building as the eaves decrease in size.

And yet in China we are faced with a conception of architecture that is fundamentally different from anything encountered so far. Elsewhere the ancient cultures and the high civilizations up to only five centuries ago (and more recently even than that)' are known and recognized chiefly by their architectural monuments and the painting, sculpture and decorative arts associated with them. The great early civilizations in particular are characterized by their monumental temple buildings, and India was no exception to this. But our knowledge of early Chinese culture—sophisticated for at least three and a half millennia—is derived largely from written sources and almost entirely without evidence from any significant architectural monuments. The earliest surviving building of any size on Chinese soil dates in its present form from the sixth century AD, and what is known of earlier buildings comes from literary sources, from pottery models, from later buildings known to be faithful reconstructions, and from buildings outside China, in Japan especially, which preserve earlier Chinese forms. This is not entirely fortuitous, but is due to a quite different approach of the Chinese, for in the development of their architecture the controlling factor was always the secular rather than the religious building, the house or palace rather than the temple. In addition, although their technical knowledge (includ-

ing the use of the arch) was more than adequate, they preferred to rely on traditional methods of construction, with extensive use of wood. This accounts for the survival of so little of any antiquity, for the Chinese had splendid towns and palaces, though not the monumental stone temple buildings familiar from other civilizations. The Great Wall is the one old stone monument of colossal dimensions, and although its present external form is only a few centuries old, it was originally begun in the third century BC and can suggest to us the extent and accomplishment of Chinese architecture in earlier periods.

The earliest surviving structures in China itself are Buddhist monuments, both rock-cut shrines, of which a number exist from the fourth century AD, in imitation of those in India, and pagodas, which served in China as an equivalent to the Indian *stupa*. In Japan, however, there exist temples of the Shinto religion, whose form dates to the third century AD, although they have been reconstructed much more recently. These are characteristically plain halls supported on a stilt structure with steeply pitched roofs and overhanging eaves. They ante-date any Chinese or Buddhist influence, and the simple construction, none of whose elements is concealed, and the use of contrasting materials with plain surfaces, conforms with a characteristic of Japanese architecture that survives throughout the period of Chinese cultural domination and is reaffirmed in Japanese buildings from the seventeenth century on.

With Buddhism Chinese influence in Japan became dominant, and although the earliest pagodas survive in China, Japan has better preserved the whole complex of the Buddhist temple. The form of the pagoda, a tiered tower made up of pavilions of similar design decreasing in size towards the top and capped by a decorated finial, was an amalgam of the important features of the Indian *stupa* and the traditional Chinese watchtower, known to us from pottery models. The earliest, the Sung Yüeh pagoda in Honan of AD 523, built of brick, is close in form to Indian models, and the famous 'Wild Goose' pagoda, built by an abbot who had undertaken a pilgrimage to India, though apparently closer to Chinese forms, was stated to have been a close copy of an Indian

model. The typical Chinese form using the traditional four-sided open pavilion for its unit and built of wood survives intact only in later versions.

Chinese architecture was traditionally urban, based on the city divided in a grid pattern with square areas made up of houses and courtyards and orientated on a central axis, on which the chief buildings stood. In the temple complex the pagoda was originally placed axially, but unlike the *stupa*, which remained the focus of Indian Buddhist architecture, the pagoda was removed quite early on from its central position, as greater emphasis came to be given to a building that conformed more closely to their town architecture. This was the great assembly hall, descended from the Indian *vihara*, which contained images of the Buddha. Two great halls survive in China dating from the T'ang period (7th to 9th centuries AD), which demonstrate a

Kuan-yin Hall, Tu-lo-ssu, Chi-hsien; *984.* The hall houses a colossal clay image of the Bodhisattva Kuan-yin, which stands on the central platform and rises through the three storeys to the canopy below the roof. The diagram clearly shows the system of wooden brackets *(tou-kung)* by which the floors, eaves and rafters are supported, demonstrating how completely the traditional architecture of China is based on post and lintel construction.

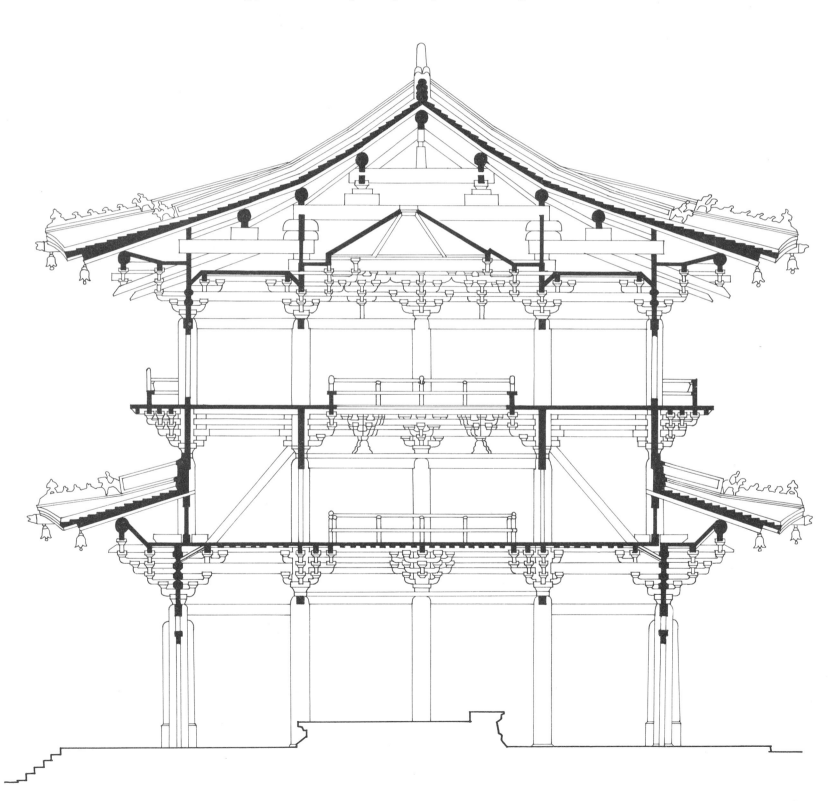

OPPOSITE **Five-storeyed pagoda, Horyu-ji;** *7th century.*
The Horyu-ji temple contains the oldest monumental architecture in wood in the world, the Kondo, or Golden Hall, and the pagoda beside it. Here too the complex bracketing system has been used to support the deeply overhanging eaves.

RIGHT **Great Buddha Hall, Todai-ji;** *c.750, reconstructed 17th century.*
The hall of the Todai-ji formed the centrepiece of the monastery, with no pagoda on the axis, but two arranged symmetrically to left and right. It was built on a huge scale (the original hall was 275 feet across), certainly in emulation of the great Chinese capitals at Ch'ang-an and Lo-yang.

BELOW **Phoenix Hall, Byodo-in;** *1053.*
Built on a quite different scale from the Hall at Todai-ji (the central hall is only 30 feet wide), it is a masterpiece of refinement, with striking use of colour in the vermilion and white decoration.

BELOW RIGHT **Tomb of General Kim Yusin, Ch'unghyo-dong, Kyongju, Korea;** *8th century.*
One of the characteristic structures of the Korean Great Silla period is the burial mound, or tumulus, surrounded by sculptured pillars with representations of the zodiac and guardian figures. The funeral mound contained in an enclosure with a strong sense of orientation is a universal form—from the pyramids to the Buddhist *stupa*.

simplicity of construction and purity of style that was never matched in later times; but these developments can best be followed in examples from Japan, where, by way of Korea, Chinese influence, including the introduction of Buddhism, became strong in the Asuka (AD 538–645) and Nara (710–784) periods. The Horyu-ji temple of the seventh century is the outstanding Asuka monument; it has a five-storeyed pagoda, in which there is no longer any trace of Indian influence, and which displays the characteristic wooden bracket system supporting the deeply overhanging roof. The tapering is extremely elegant, the roof sizes being in the proportion of 10:9:8:7:6. The Nara period in Japan received much of its inspiration from the greatness of the T'ang period in China, attempting to emulate the glories of the new capital city of Ch'ang-an, which embodied Chinese principles of town-planning on a vast scale. Some impression of the splendour of this period can be gained from the temple of Todai-ji, the Eastern Great Monastery of Nara, where the great hall was constructed to house the gigantic fifty-three-foot-high bronze statue of the Buddha. Although this is a reconstruction of the seventeenth century, it is a building of tremendous grandeur, the largest wooden building under one roof in the world.

Japanese architecture can also give us an idea of Chinese palace buildings of the T'ang and Sung (960–1279) periods. The rich ornamentation and the symmetrical layout of the Phoenix Hall in the Byodo-in monastery of the eleventh century are of Chinese origin, although its small scale and garden setting are typically Japanese, and it is indeed the greatest surviving example of the architecture of the sumptuous Fujiwara period in Japan.

Ch'ang-an was the first of the great planned Chinese cities, based on the unit of the single house, of which the courtyard is an integral part, designed symmetrically with the entrance on the axis. These houses were grouped together in a *fang*, the square formed by the intersection of streets arranged on a grid plan. Chinese cities of mature design were not formed by the gradual additions of new *fangs* as the population increased, but were built from the start, on a roughly square grid with a north–south axis, to accommodate a maximum population, and these people were recruited into the city from the surrounding countryside. The whole city was surrounded by a wall, with formidable gates, particularly at the point where the main axial street met the north and south walls. This arrangement dominates Chinese architecture and is applied to almost every com-

RIGHT **Houses in Peking.** These show the rectangular divisions filled with narrow one-storey buildings fronting on courtyards.

BELOW **Throne Hall, or Hall of Supreme Harmony, Forbidden City, Peking;** *c.1700.* Despite its comparatively late date, the hall is based on traditional Ming models. It stands on a triple terrace of marble as the most imposing of all the buildings on the great central square of the Forbidden City.

BOTTOM **Liu Yüan (Lingering Garden), Suchow;** *16th century.* The latticed windows of the buildings and their decorative roofs create a harmony both of scale and of form with the natural surroundings.

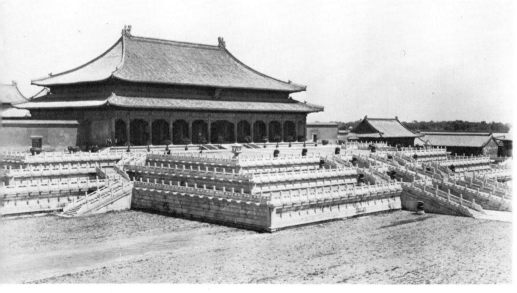

plex of buildings. It is analogous to the plan of Egyptian or Hindu temples, but although the most important buildings were normally situated on the axis, each individual house reflected the plan of the whole city and had its independent focus, without reference to the central point to which, in the temples elsewhere, all attention was directed. Ch'ang-an did not survive the end of the T'ang dynasty (*c.* 900), and the Chinese city plan is seen at its most perfect in Peking, which became the capital city of the Chinese Empire during the fourteenth century.

There had been several earlier cities on the site of Peking, built on the grid pattern, but its present form dates from the reconstructions in the fifteenth and sixteenth centuries after it had finally become the capital city of the Ming emperors. The axial plan is strongly accented and at the city's centre is the 'Forbidden City' of the Imperial family, with a succession of gates and halls on its main axis. This is perhaps the most impressive palace in the world, of emperors who considered all other rulers their vassals. It is surrounded by walls with massive fortified gate houses, and progress along the axial avenue is repeatedly interrupted by more gates or

halls. On approaching the centre, the architecture becomes more intimate and at the same time more richly decorated, and is constructed of precious materials, with extensive use of white marble. It is, as much as Indian architecture, a complex to move through, but whereas the great Indian shrines were places of pilgrimage, places to seek the centre of the world, the Chinese placed themselves at the centre and built out from it. The Forbidden City is a practical exposition of this concept.

In comparison, the chief religious monument of Peking is of an astonishing simplicity. This is the complex of the Temple and Altar of Heaven, consisting of a succession of temples and halls on a long broad avenue leading to the altar, a mound surrounded by four circular balustrades within a vast square precinct. Again it is in the progression towards the most purified form that the beauty and the sophistication lie. This is also due in part to the landscape setting, the vast park in which the buildings are contained, for in China, as in Japan, a major role is played by landscape in architecture. This may seem at variance with the formal layout of the cities, but there had always been a most sophisticated

appreciation of landscape, as can be seen both from Chinese paintings and poetry. The artificial gardens in cities and villas are designed to give a greater variation of sublime natural beauty than would even be found in nature itself and to combine it with picturesque architecture. The most celebrated of the Chinese town gardens, apart from the Summer Palace in Peking, of which little survives in its original form, is at Suchow, famous since Mongol times, but reaching its present form in the Ming period, and harmoniously combining trees, water and architecture in a composition of wonderful refinement.

In Japan the garden villa was of great antiquity, and here in its final sophistication Japanese architecture becomes subject to nature, returning to the simplest forms with natural materials that was the native Japanese style from earliest times. The imperial garden villa of Katsura, dating from the seventeenth century, epitomizes the style of architecture and decoration that relates furnishings to the interior architecture and both to the exterior and to its setting. It was an ideal not to be achieved in European architecture until the mid-twentieth century.

Rooms in the New Palace, Katsura Imperial Villa; *17th century*. Built in three stages by Prince Toshihito and his successor Prince Toshitada, Katsura Villa is the outstanding example of Japanese domestic architecture; it is composed of a number of buildings, asymmetrically planned and set in a garden traditionally ascribed to the great tea-master Kobori Enshu (1577–1647). The proportions of the interiors are based on the unit of the mat, and the most elaborate attention was paid to the graining of wood and other details of texture.

CHAPTER 7

REVIVALS

OPPOSITE **Library, Kenwood, Hampstead;** *R. Adam, 1767–8.* Although Adam drew heavily on many ancient sources—Roman, Etruscan, Gothic, etc.—for his forms and for his decoration, he was concerned with their appropriateness and adapted them to suit their situation. He thought the attention paid to the Orders was 'frequently minute' and considered the use of Roman temple architecture in the living room, ridiculous, attacking architects who used 'massive entablatures', 'ponderous compartment ceilings' or a cornice 'fit for the temple of Jupiter Tonans, from which it was probably copied'.

By the middle of the eighteenth century architects had seemed unable to take Renaissance styles any further and two opposing developments had emerged, the one highly decorative, with extensive use of painting and sculpture and little interest in architectural structures, adopting anything from alien cultures that would appeal to the taste for the picturesque, the other looking back to the monumental Classicism of the High Renaissance and of Antiquity, with the subordination of all decorative elements to structural necessity. Both were strongly derivative and they represented the opposing poles of taste in Europe. But in the increasingly revolutionary climate of thought in the second half of the century architectural style was no longer a matter of taste or fashion; along with the other fine arts, architecture became considered a moral and social force for good or evil, and the consideration of this was a prime function of the architect. Architectural forms and structures had to be 'natural'; and so the theorists considered *chinoiserie* depraving, while Classical architecture was at first seen as the embodiment of nature in its highest and truest form. (The idea that architecture should be natural—true to itself and true to its function—has never since been abandoned, but the architectural history of the past two centuries shows how illusory is this ideal; each successive movement has given it a new meaning, and moral rather than aesthetic arguments have been used to justify the building of much that is ugly and inappropriate and the neglect and even destruction of much that was decorative and beautiful—though in recent years still more fine buildings have fallen victim to arguments of expediency.)

In England the Palladian movement and in France the increasingly Classicizing architecture of Gabriel had anticipated the Neo-Classical ideal of natural architecture, and the Paris church of Ste Geneviève (the Panthéon) by Gabriel's younger contemporary Jacques-Germain Soufflot (1713–80) is quite deliberately based on a post and lintel construction, 'natural' in its avoidance of arches which spring directly from columns. The same return to Classical models without any Renaissance intermediary can be seen in the work of the Scottish architect Robert Adam (1728–92), whose work was strongly inspired by archeological sources, which included the recently discovered interior decoration of Pompeii and Herculaneum as well as the antiquities of Rome. Adam's Classicism was presented as a living style; his interiors have neither the sculptural decoration of the Baroque, nor the restlessness of Rococo, but use muted pastel colours, with flat plaster moulding and, in some instances, circular and oval painted panels set in walls or ceilings—but employing no Baroque false perspectives. The library at Kenwood House, with stucco by Joseph Rose, shows, as well as a masterly handling of space, with apsed form and coved ceiling, Adam's sense of colour and his ability to give richness to a

decorative scheme without its becoming either ostentatious or overpowering. Adam's near-contemporary William Chambers (1723–96), with whom his name is often coupled, remained more firmly in the Anglo-Palladian tradition. Whether working on the massive scale of Somerset House on the Thames Embankment or in miniature, as at the Casina at Marino, Dublin, Chambers's style is derived from the legacy of Wren and Vanbrugh and the buildings of Colen Campbell

RIGHT **Toll-house of la Villette, Paris;** *C. N. Ledoux, 1785–9.* Ledoux's buildings show the clearly defined volumes and simple structures of pure Neo-Classicism, but this is almost a lost style; its starkness (and the colossal scale of many projects) led to very few commissions. BELOW **Panthéon, Paris;** *J. G. Soufflot; begun 1757.* Soufflot studied new methods of construction and, as well as being a prototype of Neo-Classicism, the Panthéon offers one of the earliest examples of the use of iron to reinforce an architectural structure.

and William Kent, though his admiration of Soufflot led to a greater refinement in his work.

Two of America's most notable architects, Thomas Jefferson (1743–1826) and Charles Bulfinch (1763–1844), also travelled to Italy and introduced the influence of Classicism to the United States. Both remained deeply indebted to English styles, and Jefferson's own house at Monticello is of obvious Palladian inspiration, while the Boston churches of Bulfinch are derived directly from the work of Wren and Gibbs. The fine houses of Samuel McIntyre (1757–1811) at Salem, Mass., also follow traditional models, though some of his later work shows the influence of Adam styles. But Jefferson's University of Virginia at Charlottesville, with its long colonnade leading to the central Palladian rotunda, and even more his new Virginia State Capitol at Richmond, which is directly inspired by Classical temple design, show evidence of the Classical Revival. The same is true of Bulfinch's Massachusetts State House, in its time the most imposing public building in the United States. The façade leads up from a rusticated basement through austere brick arcades, a long marble colonnade and a brick and marble pediment to the gilt dome. The colonnade, which dominates the façade, seems to be based on the peristyle of a Classical temple, with its pediment, in perfect proportion, raised above it and turned through ninety degrees. Throughout the nineteenth century the Greek or Roman temple was to dominate the design of parliament and other public buildings, and these early examples ingeniously integrate this with the Palladian tradition.

The Neo-Classical pursuit of naturalism was taken to its limits in France, where Classical forms were refined by reducing them to the simplest geometrical elements, very clearly articulated, in contrast to the spatial ambiguities of the Baroque. The visionary and megalomaniac projects of Étienne-Louis Boullée (1728–99), hardly any of whose designs were executed, included gigantic spherical structures (up to five hundred feet high) shorn of all Classical detailing, but the works of Claude-Nicolas Ledoux (1736–1806) exemplify the ideals of the theorists in the pure forms of his Paris toll-houses and the monumental grandeur of the ideal village—not fully carried out—attached to the salt-works at Arc-et-Senans. In the Napoleonic era these new directions were largely stultified and public architecture throughout Napoleon's empire was characterized by a display of ostentation and gigantism, which became familiar in this century as the architectural idiom of dictatorship.

However a style originates, whether by a process of straightforward development or as a result of intellectual theories, there will be architects who simply adopt it for their buildings as the fashionable style. The picturesque eclecticism of the eighteenth century had not been entirely superseded by Neo-Classicism, which itself, as time went on, tended more and more to become simply a Greek Revival style. Then other historical styles began to be revived too, and the theory was developed—which really came into its own in mid-century—that a particular historical or exotic style was specially appropriate for a particular type of building. Throughout the nineteenth century there were architects who built up an extensive repertory of styles, none more fluently than John Nash (1752–1835), whose rebuilding of the Royal Pavilion at Brighton for the Prince Regent in 1815 made of it a real 'pleasure-dome' in a mock-Indian (Indian Gothic it was called at the time) style reminiscent of the nabobs of *Vanity Fair*. Elsewhere Nash used Gothic and rustic styles, though it is his Renaissance and Grecian terraces in London on which his fame rests, the best surviving being those around Regent's Park.

LEFT **Monticello, Va.;**
T. Jefferson, c. 1770–1800.
It was through Palladio
that Jefferson discovered
Antiquity, and his own
work shows that he
continued to see Ancient
buildings to some extent
through Palladian eyes.

BELOW LEFT
**Massachusetts State
House, Boston;**
C. Bulfinch, 1795–1800.
The measured Palladianism
of the State House shows
the influence of Chambers's
Somerset House in London.

BOTTOM LEFT
**Schoongezicht, near
Cape Town;** *gables 1813.*
Cape homesteads show a
colonial survival of the
Dutch gable, developed for
the narrow street fronts of
17th-century town houses.

BELOW **Royal Pavilion,
Brighton;** *J. Nash, 1815.*
Nash made extensive use of
iron at Brighton: the dome
has a cast iron substructure
weighing 60 tons, and the
kitchen roof rests on cast
iron columns terminating
in decorative palm fronds.

The Mausoleum, Dulwich Art Gallery;
Sir J. Soane, 1811–14.
The simple, clear-cut forms of Soane's architecture are often compared to the contemporary work of Thomas Telford and other engineer-architects, but Soane's work is a great deal more subtle, and it is not a comparison he would have relished himself—having written that he hoped 'that our great Public and Private works will no longer be entrusted to ignorant mechanics . . .'.

BELOW LEFT **Cathedral of Our Lady, Copenhagen;**
C. F. Hansen, 1810–29.
The massive Doric colonnade and the coffered barrel vault give a sense of great monumentality.
BELOW RIGHT **Admiralty, St Petersburg;**
A. D. Zakharov, 1806–15.
The Admiralty was one of many Neo-Classical buildings by Russians and foreigners in St Petersburg. This main entrance shows the massive effect of the superimposed cubes countered by the more traditional lantern and spire.

It was the Grecian style—more limited, but purer and more 'natural' than Roman—that dominated the first decades of the new century, though there were still architects whose work was closer to the simple geometric, non-historical ideal of Neo-Classicism, notably the very personal contribution of Sir John Soane (1753–1837) in England and the buildings of the influential C. F. Hansen (1756–1845) in Denmark. Neither architect entirely abandoned Renaissance language. Soane's preference for the Ionic Order and his careful articulation of the elements employed give many of his buildings an intimacy unusual at this period; but Hansen's severe Doric and stark, rather massive forms are in marked contrast to the joyous—if less 'responsible'—handling of the Classical Orders a hundred years before by the successors of Bernini and Borromini. Wherever the Baroque had flourished most vigorously, the new style awakened least response. Its most fruitful ground was the Protestant north, and it found its greatest exponents in Prussia. Here it became a true expression of the Romantic movement, first of all in the heroic Classicism of the short-lived Friedrich Gilly (1772–1800), who exerted a wide influence, though he completed no building of significance. C. F. Hansen represents one strain of this, but more significant is the work of the greatest architect of the age, Karl Friedrich Schinkel (1781–1841). Schinkel studied under Gilly, but spent the years between Gilly's death in 1800 and 1815, when he was put in charge of the Prussian Office of Public Works, in travelling, painting and working on the design of furniture. He contributed greatly to the development of Berlin in the early nineteenth century, working initially in a strict Grecian style. His Old Museum in Berlin shows a deep understanding of the use of columns and

entablatures to define the proportions of the simple geometrical forms. Later, Schinkel adopted, with comparable success, other styles, Gothic and Romanesque for churches, and for a number of buildings a simplified monumental style, which was to transmit the influence of Neo-Classicism to the early architects of the Modern Movement at the beginning of the twentieth century. Schinkel's Grecian style was also successfully adopted in southern Germany by Leo von Klenze, who worked in Munich and elsewhere.

The development of the city of Berlin was paralleled in other great cities, as the Industrial Revolution and the coming of railways accelerated the move away from the countryside. London grew faster than any and the fields of villages like Kensington, Islington and Lambeth were covered with squares and terraces built by speculators. The quality of the building was often poor, and much even of John Nash's great scheme—employing a variety of Classical styles, but broadly in the tradition of the Woods of Bath—going from Piccadilly Circus to Regent's Park has been demolished and what remains has had to be partly reconstructed. As in Berlin, the important commissions were for public buildings—the British Museum, the National Gallery, London University (now University College) and many others—rather than for private palaces. But many new churches were built for the swarming population, most following the plan established by Wren, Hawksmoor and Gibbs, though this was occasionally combined successfully with a more archeologically exact rendering of Classical detail. W. and H. W. Inwood's church of St Pancras is in the form of an Ionic temple, with acanthus cresting all round, with an apse and with two vestries at the side decorated with caryatids modelled on those from the Erechtheum in Athens (*see* p. 25). The octagonal shape of the tower, freely based on Greek models, is carried down into a corresponding vestibule in the interior, while the body of the church is in a pure and light Grecian style to match the exterior.

The greatest American master of the Grecian style was Benjamin H. Latrobe (1764–1820), whose semicircular Hall of Representatives in Washington and wide domed cathedral in Baltimore are works of great monumentality. Their influence was widespread and remained alive well into the twentieth century, when Classical Revival buildings were still being designed and constructed.

ABOVE **Old Museum, Berlin;** *K. F. Schinkel, 1823–8.*
The main hall is domed inside, and the interior arrangement of the galleries is carefully devised to display both sculpture and paintings effectively.
LEFT **St Pancras parish church, London;** *W. and H. W. Inwood, 1818–22.*
BELOW **Roman Catholic Cathedral, Baltimore;** *B. Latrobe, 1805–18.*
The cathedral shows Latrobe's strong feeling for the geometry of space, with limited use of the Orders.

Royal Throne, House of Lords, Westminster; *A. W. Pugin, 1844–52.* Pugin's superb Gothic decorative scheme in the House of Lords was one of the most extravagant and—in a sense—one of the most fitting achievements of Victorian revivalism. Yet it still requires a great effort of the imagination to understand fully why a style four or five hundred years old should have been thought appropriate even for a building designed to serve such a traditional function.

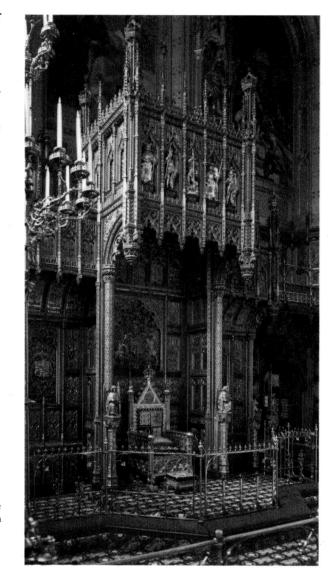

BELOW **Keble College, Oxford;** *W. Butterfield, begun 1868.* Butterfield's Gothic is far less literally transcribed from the Middle Ages than Pugin's, and made its effect more by richness of colour than by sculptural detail. His work was mainly in the service of the high Anglican Oxford Movement and was intended to provide a fitting setting for their life and ritual.

But already before 1850 the same objections were being raised to Greek styles as had been earlier to the hedonistic architecture of the eighteenth century—that they were unnatural. In the ensuing 'Battle of the Styles' the opposing factions were the advocates of natural forms and those of Classic forms (who considered that these *were* natural forms). To start with, at least, natural forms were generally taken to mean Gothic, and the Gothic Revivalists looked back nostalgically to the Christian Middle Ages, a period that seemed to them pure, devout and true to itself. Their enthusiasm was parodied by Dickens, whose Mrs Skewton is reminded by Warwick Castle of 'those darling byegone times, with their delicious fortresses, and their dear old dungeons, and their delightful places of torture, and their romantic vengeances, and their picturesque assaults and sieges, and everything that makes life truly charming! How dreadfully we have degenerated!' The leading apostle of the Gothic Revival was Augustus Welby Pugin (1812–52), who built fine churches and a number of private houses, as well as playing a major role in the architecture of the British Houses of Parliament.

But the battle between Gothic and Classicism was only one aspect, and the picturesque eclecticism of Nash was taken up with greater earnestness, so that throughout the western world the bewildering question 'What style should this be built in?' was answered 'Whatever style is most appropriate to its place and function.' In England it was decided that for the new Houses of Parliament the 'national' style should be adopted, considered to be the Perpendicular Gothic of late Plantagenet and early Tudor times. The design was prepared by Sir Charles Barry (1795–1860), who carried it out with the help of Pugin. Barry had already undertaken some small London churches in Gothic, as well as a Grecian art gallery, but his best building had been the Travellers' Club in London, where he used a new Neo-Renaissance style, based on fifteenth-century models. Later he was to employ a variant of this, based on sixteenth-century styles, with still greater success for the Reform Club, a brilliant pastiche of an Italian *palazzo*. Both buildings influenced innumerable works of lesser quality in the Italianate style. The overall plan of the Houses of Parliament, in university collegiate rather than ecclesiastical Gothic, was Barry's, and with its long riverside façade and balanced towers and spires it is one of the most successful—and certainly one of the most beloved—monumental buildings of the nineteenth century. It is indicative of Barry's ease with styles that one could well visualize the same buildings carried out with Renaissance rather than Gothic detailing. The Gothic was the work of Pugin, and especially in the interiors, such as the royal throne in the House of Lords, this is of astonishing richness.

The theory of architecture's moral value was never so explicitly propounded as by the English Gothic Revivalists, who saw medieval styles as a symbol of the lost innocence of the Middle Ages, which they hoped to regain in religion and in life by creating Gothic surroundings in which to live and work, and this took in furniture and many household objects as well as buildings. The most individual architect of the group—which besides Pugin included J. L. Pearson and the influential G. E. Street—was William Butterfield (1814–1900), whose works are remarkable for their vivid effects of colour. The use of polychrome bricks enlivened his buildings, though with little regard for their surroundings, and his chapel for the new foundation of Keble College, Oxford, which is a masterpiece of proportion and Gothic detail, looks garish amid the weathered honey-coloured stone of the older colleges.

Street's most important work was the Law Courts in

The Red House, Bexleyheath; *P. Webb, 1859–60.*
The Red House belongs to the Gothic Revival, although there is no attempt to apply ecclesiastical Gothic to a domestic dwelling (no more appropriate and often a lot less convenient than Greek temple architecture in the same context). But neither is this picturesque rustic architecture as practised in the late 18th century and by Nash; the asymmetrical layout and free forms of the house arise from inner necessity and convenience, giving people priority over appearances.

RIGHT **Marseilles Cathedral;** *L. Vaudoyer, 1852.*
A typical example of the many local revival styles in Europe. The larger the scale, the harder it seems to have been to give a spark of life to buildings constructed according to an overall plan, whose models had an organic growth that often extended over centuries.

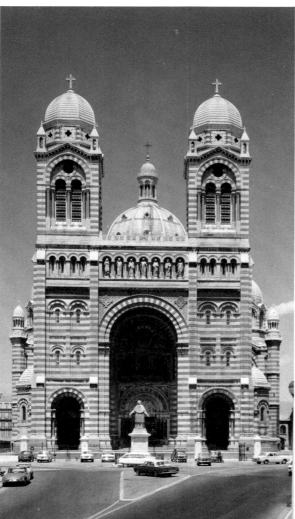

London, but his significance lies rather in his pupils, who included William Morris, Philip Webb and Richard Norman Shaw. William Morris (1834–96) took the concept of naturalism a step further, not seeing it in terms of the battle of the styles, but as the fight for craftsmanship in the increasingly industrial age. His inspiration was behind the Arts and Crafts Movement, which wanted to preserve this tradition. The Red House built for him by Philip Webb (1831–1915) rejected the decorative elements of a particular style and reverted to the long tradition of English domestic building. The house was true to itself and true to its practical rather than its representative function, and as such it is a revolutionary and pioneering work. Morris's efforts were paralleled in the United States by the theories of the landscape architect Andrew Downing (1815–52), who advocated building private houses to look like cottages rather than miniature Greek temples.

But for some time to come Gothic was effectively unchallenged, at least when it was felt apt for a particular type of building, though outside England other national forms of the style were used. In France, where the influence of the architect, theorist, restorer extraordinary and medievalist Eugène-Emmanuel Viollet-le-Duc (1814–79) was paramount, a 'Romano-Byzantine' style was among those favoured for ecclesiastical buildings, deriving in part from the Romanesque domed churches of central France, at Périgeux, Le Puy and elsewhere; the most famous example is the Sacré-Coeur basilica at Montmartre, though more successful is Marseilles Cathedral by Léon Vaudoyer (1803–72).

The industrial age, against which William Morris reacted so strongly, had a powerful effect on architecture. To start with it had created the most dramatic developments in civil engineering—in the construction of canals, railways, bridges, viaducts—and then in industrial architecture—docks, railway stations and factories; it had transformed the towns and cities into vast urban areas, whose real housing needs were not even considered humanely for another century, in spite of philanthropic estates and blocks of flats; and it had introduced new methods of construction, which were open to architects to develop. The first to take advantage of these were, naturally enough, the engineers, and the bridges and dock buildings of Thomas Telford (1757–1834) are much admired for the way in which their simplicity anticipates the architecture of the late nineteenth and twentieth centuries. But these were not so much selfconscious architecture as triumphs of engineering—and were admired by contemporaries as

such. Nevertheless, the use of iron and glass as building materials was extended, and from the eighteen-twenties covered arcades of shops were built, and also market halls. But it was with the covered engine sheds of railway stations that these constructions made their greatest impression in the cities—apart from the *tour de force* of Joseph Paxton's Crystal Palace, built for the Great Exhibition of 1851 in Hyde Park, and based on hothouse design.

The double standard towards architecture and engineering is exemplified in the building for St Pancras Station and Hotel in London. It was one of the later railway stations to be built, but the engineer W. H. Barlow (1812–1902) covered the platforms with an iron and glass vault spanning 243 feet, still the largest in Europe, not in a pure curve but forming a shallow pointed arch. This and a little Gothic detailing in the cast-iron brackets were the only concessions to conventional aesthetic rather than purely constructional considerations. But

ABOVE **Museum of Science (detail), Oxford;** *B. Woodward, 1855–8.* From the mid-century iron became increasingly used in conjunction with masonry. 'The difficulty,' wrote a contemporary of the museum, 'was to do this without limiting the design to the many structural features of the Crystal Palace or condescending to the vulgar detail of a railway terminus.'

ABOVE **Bibliothèque Ste Geneviève, Paris;** *H. Labrouste, 1843–50.* Labrouste was one of the first architects to reject decisively the French establishment under the Académie des Beaux-Arts. He showed great boldness in the iron constructions of his two Paris libraries, and there is nothing of the rather pedantic revivalism of Woodward's museum.
LEFT **Parliamentary Library, Ottawa;** *Thomas Fuller and C. Jones, 1859–67.* Gothic Revival buildings were to be found throughout the Victorian Empire. The Ottawa library is a beautifully proportioned building, modelled closely on a medieval chapter house, on a much enlarged scale.

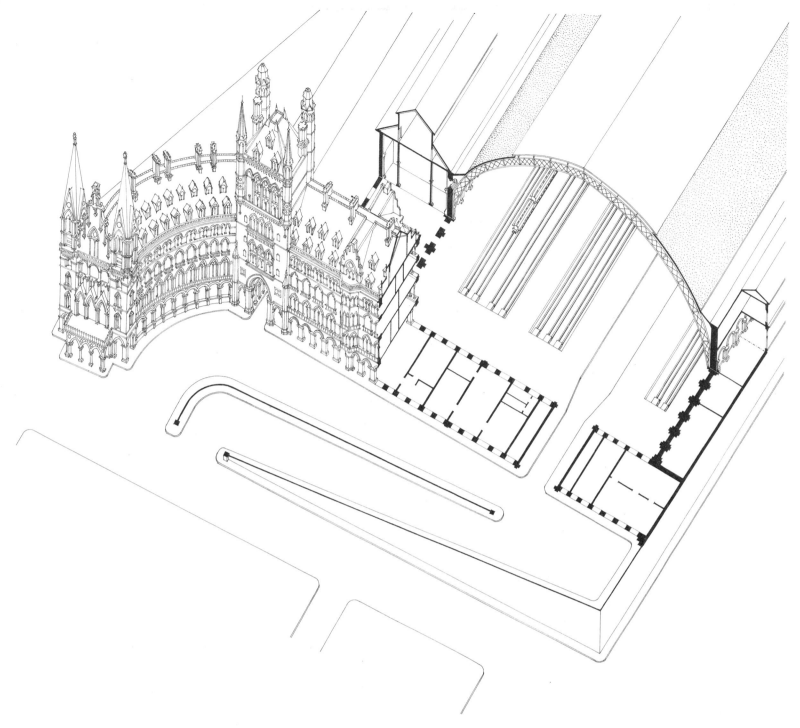

the station building itself and the adjoining hotel, which carries on the façade round a curve, are in unrestrained red-brick Gothic trimmed with white sandstone and pink granite. Its designer was Sir George Gilbert Scott (1811–78), the most prolific of the mid-Victorian Gothic architects (he is said to have been responsible for nearly eight hundred buildings), and St Pancras, with its capitals carved with railway officials and workmen and its magnificent iron double staircase in the hotel, is one of the most picturesque monuments of the age.

While St Pancras shows little attempt to harmonize architecture and engineering, in mid-century there were a number of architects who did just that. In particular, two of the greatest artistic theorists of the nineteenth century, Ruskin and Viollet-le-Duc attempted a reconciliation. John Ruskin (1819–1900), who had no use for the Crystal Palace, shared Morris's admiration of the craftsmanship of the Middle Ages and the fellowship of those craftsmen; he spurned the industrial age, and he too was a major inspiration to the influential Arts and Crafts Movement. But in Oxford, the metropolis of the Gothic Revival, he supervised the construction of the Museum of Science, designed by Benjamin Woodward (1815–61) in the 'Veronese' Gothic style, using an

iron and glass roof, supported on iron columns, decorated with superb cast-iron capitals with naturalistic flower, leaf and fruit designs, based on the medieval cathedral carvings of Lincoln or Southwell. In France Viollet-le-Duc was also fascinated by the possibilities offered by the new materials and constructional techniques, and the designs in his influential treatise, the *Entretiens sur l'Architecture* (1863–72) make comparisons between the skeleton constructions of the Gothic cathedrals and those possible with the use of iron.

Several contemporaries of Viollet-le-Duc did make substantial use of iron and glass within conventional buildings, and in the two Paris libraries, the Bibliothèque Nationale and the Bibliothèque Ste Geneviève, by Vaudoyer's pupil Henri Labrouste (1801–75), unlike Woodward's Gothic in Oxford, a Classical style was attempted, the former having very tall attenuated columns surmounted by Corinthian capitals to support the multiple domes. Masonry and iron were also combined in buildings in the Low Countries, and the Bourse in Antwerp by J. H. M. Schadde (1818–94) shows the technique married to a rich late Gothic styling, based on the fifteenth-century commercial style of the Netherlands.

St Pancras Station, London; *train shed, W. H. Barlow, 1863, station and hotel, Sir G. G. Scott, 1866–7.* Barlow's work is of great historical importance; earlier he had worked with Paxton on the Crystal Palace, one of the first constructions to be made of prefabricated standardized parts, for which Barlow calculated the required strength. St Pancras was the first hall of iron and glass to use a continuous arch without distinction between 'walls' and 'roof', anticipating by more than twenty years the more famous Hall of Machines at the 1889 exhibition in Paris. Scott's building reflects the style in which he had hoped to rebuild the Whitehall ministries.

Opéra, Paris; *C. Garnier, 1861–75.*
The Opéra, with its grand staircase of Algerian onyx, marks the high point of the sumptuous style of the French Second Empire. It is over-elaborate display architecture, the acoustics are left to chance (unlike the Wagner theatre at Bayreuth, where Semper demonstrated the success of a scientific approach to the problem)—and yet it is one of the most beloved monuments of Paris.

Burgtheater, Vienna; *G. Semper and Karl von Hasenauer, 1880–6.* This is probably the best of the rich variety of buildings on the Ringstrasse and is a fine example of the favoured Italian Renaissance style. Semper realized that revivalist styles would soon have had their day, writing that 'the key task of the art industry of the future is the destruction of the old traditional forms.'

Although 'national' styles were often preferred, by the second half of the century a whole repertory of historical styles, which was continually being enlarged, had become available to architects throughout Europe. It was an equivalent of the un-Classical Italianate style that Barry had used so successfully in his London clubs that seemed most appropriate for town houses, theatres, clubs, hotels—for all buildings associated with the social world rather than for public or ecclesiastical purposes. The extensive campaigns of rebuilding in the city centres of Paris and Vienna in the sixties and seventies exemplify this. In Paris Napoleon III commissioned Baron Haussmann (1809–91) to demolish and reconstruct a large part of the old city, and taking the Arc de Triomphe as a focus Haussmann built twelve radiating boulevards, the main one, the Champs Elysées, leading down to the obelisk in the Place de la Concorde, the vista continuing through the Tuileries Gardens to the Louvre Palace. The plan was a magnificent one and the tree-lined boulevards were flanked with grand town houses built in a French dialect of the Neo-Renaissance style. Although many architects collaborated on the detailed designs, the most important single contribution was made by Charles Garnier (1825–98), both by his Neo-Baroque building for the Opéra, which was indebted to Venetian styles for its architectural detail and in its extreme luxury of decoration and use of extravagant materials, and by his development of the luxury apartment, well planned and with finely proportioned rooms. Increasingly in every major city in the west the flat or apartment was to become the normal unit of family accommodation across a broad class spectrum, and Garnier's contribution to its development was crucial.

In Vienna too Neo-Renaissance buildings outnumbered those in other styles, but here a far more complete exposition of the eclectic use of historical styles is to be found, since so many more major public buildings were erected. It was finally decided in 1857 to remove the old fortifications, thus clearing a wide space all round the central city on which a single boulevard, the Ringstrasse, was planned. Around this, monumental new public buildings were to be constructed, each in a style appropriate to its function, and many of the architects involved showed an astonishing versatility. The Parliament building was Grecian, by Theophil Hansen (1813–91, son of the Neo-Classicist C. F. Hansen), whose Exchange and Musikverein concert-hall were in early Renaissance style—with Grecian elements—but who also had a hand in designing the new Arsenal, a fortified Neo-Romanesque building. The Votive Church was built in purest French High Gothic and the University in Franco-Italian Renaissance, both by Heinrich Ferstel (1828–83), the most prolific of the Viennese Neo-Renaissance architects, who also intro-

RIGHT **Staircase, Château-sur-Mer, Newport, R.I.;**
R. M. Hunt, remodelled 1872.
While Europe was building grand public architecture, the American 'robber barons' wanted their private houses built on the grand scale, and Newport became a battle-ground as millionaires tried to outshine their fellow millionaires. R. M. Hunt, hailed as the 'founder of the American Renaissance', was the most successful architect of the period.

BELOW **Passage by Singers' Hall, Neuschwanstein;**
Christian Jank, c.1872.
In the castles of King Ludwig II no expense was spared to recreate the unreal dream world of German medieval romance. This is vividly colourful, visionary architecture (the part shown being in Romanesque-Byzantine style), but it cannot finally be seen as anything but the most monumental folly.

duced Romanesque elements into his National Bank design. The Town Hall is Brabantine Gothic and the Academic High School English Gothic with open-beam roof, both by Friedrich von Schmidt (1825–91). The Court Theatre, the National Museums and the proposed extension to the Imperial Palace, all Neo-Renaissance tending to Neo-Baroque, were in part the work of Gottfried Semper (1803–79), probably the greatest architect of the period, and these buildings show far more concern for considerations of architectural space, of overall planning and of balanced proportions. Like Barry, Semper was not hampered by the historical styles, nor was he a slavish copyist, but was able to design freely and harmoniously within the idiom.

Vienna offers the clearest example of the theory of eclectic architecture, but everywhere suitable styles were adopted, frequently with absurd results, as when a 'national' monumental or ecclesiastical style was chosen for a country villa, though there is no denying the grandeur achieved when work was undertaken on the scale of the castles of King Ludwig II of Bavaria. Such heights of fantasy were never achieved in the work of the American Richard Morris Hunt (1827–95), trained in Paris and for decades the darling of the New York plutocracy. If he had a certain prejudice in favour of French Neo-Renaissance, that did not prevent him trying his hand at any other style that a client might require, and he almost always achieved a result both successful in itself—according to its lights—and satisfactory to his client. He flattered them. They liked to live in an Italian *palazzo,* or have a drawing room furnished in Louis XV style with genuine objects of royal pedigree, and this was a tradition that long outlived Hunt and is not totally extinct even today. But philandering with styles was in the end no substitute for the forms that were dictated by essential architectural requirements, and the stylistic detailing of past ages was not going to be the answer for buildings to serve new purposes, to be built by new methods of construction and find a place in a new environment.

Even so, it was through historical styles that the beginnings of modern architecture developed. In England Richard Norman Shaw (1831–1912), the fellow pupil with Morris and Webb of G. E. Street, pursued a career in some ways similar to Hunt's, trying his hand at a wide variety of styles, though with the significant difference that they were, almost without exception, of native and domestic origin. Though many of his 'Tudor', 'Jacobean' and 'Queen Anne' houses, both in town and country, are of extreme extravagance, sometimes even involving the most unlikely mixtures of these and other styles, when working on a less lavish scale, he

kept alive the simple tradition of Webb's Red House, and he was also responsible for the first 'Garden City' project, at Bedford Park in Chiswick, London.

Increasingly towards the end of the century local styles were chosen in European countries in preference to the ubiquitous Grecian, Gothic and Neo-Renaissance, or were at least combined with them. In the colonial territories, too, individual variants, sometimes of great charm, were evolved (*see* p. 11), and this development was paralleled in the United States, where Andrew Downing's influence began to take effect. The specifically American element in architecture that was singled out for special development was the use of rugged natural materials—rough masonry and wood in every form, for construction, in clapboarding, half-timbering and shingles—and these materials were incorporated into an equally down-to-earth form, the cottage, although it was often enlarged way beyond its normal size. The greatest exponent of this style was Henry Hobson Richardson (1838–86), who had studied in Paris under Labrouste and whose 'cottages' rubbed shoulders with Hunt's *palazzi* in Newport, R.I. But it is the development of Richardson's work from here that is so significant, since it made a decisive step towards a new style which was to establish the American leadership in architecture, undisputed in the twentieth century. In his more monumental buildings Richardson concentrated on the massive masonry, not used for picturesque effect but integrated into a suitably massive style that owes much to—or at least has much in common with—the town palaces of the Florentine Renaissance, with their heavy rustication, while its specific forms are derived rather from Romanesque. In his—now demolished—Marshall Field Warehouse in Chicago, and equally in the works of his most important successor in Chicago, Louis Sullivan (1856–1924), revivalism has been brought back to the point where it is simply monumental and non-historical, as in the work of the engineers in the first half of the century or as achieved in a few works by Sir John Soane and the romantic-classic Schinkel. Sullivan and Adler's Auditorium building in Chicago is on a massive scale, but the articulation of the façade, with heavy rustication at the lower levels, the

deep cut window surrounds covering four floors, and the scaling down of the window sizes on the topmost floors, has all the essential elements of the Florentine town palaces, without any of the—now inappropriate —stylistic details.

The activity of the Chicago school culminated in the first skyscrapers, made possible by the exploitation of steel-frame construction and the invention of the electric elevator. Some of the most striking examples were the result of the partnership of D. H. Burnham (1846–1912) and J. W. Root (1850–91), the second of whom was the great innovator, and whose Reliance Building in Chicago, begun in 1890, is faced with white tiles. The external appearance of the early skyscrapers was dictated by their construction; the impression they made and their beauty came from sheer height and from the simple, dignified way in which the exterior was handled; it was enough for them to be what they were.

As the century neared its end, the search for a style was over. Not that eclectic styles were abandoned; they continued for another half-century, but they were overshadowed by styles developed from the essential characteristics of the buildings and their construction. The superficial equation of style and function exemplified by the buildings of the Vienna Ringstrasse was superseded and it was in a very different sense that Louis Sullivan wrote 'Form follows function', and his pupil Frank Lloyd Wright said 'Form and function are one.'

ABOVE **Auditorium Building, Chicago;**
L. Sullivan and D. Adler, 1886–9.
The 'Romanesque' form of the Auditorium owes much to the influence of Richardson, and it is interesting to compare its clean lines with the Fine Arts Building on its immediate right by S. S. Beman. Although the exterior walls are of load-bearing masonry, there is an interior framing of cast and wrought iron members.
LEFT **Carson, Pirie, Scott Store, Chicago;**
L. Sullivan, 1899–1904.
Sullivan's building (though added to in the upper storeys) shows the Chicago school at its most forward-looking. It is a steel-frame construction, and this is made to dictate its form, with a repeated pattern of windows on the upper floors and an ornate screen of bronze and glass which serves as the store-front.

CHAPTER 8

MODERN MOVEMENTS

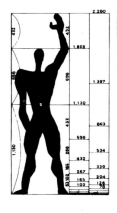

OPPOSITE **Church of the Sagrada Familia (detail), Barcelona;** *A. Gaudí, begun 1884.*
The architecture of the 19th century had been dominated by the imposition of rigid forms—Grecian, Gothic, etc.—on buildings, and one of the revolutions of modern architecture was the freedom from this constraint, so that the building was developed from the inside outwards, and decoration was allowed to take free forms. Gaudí's work typifies the most extreme sculptural approach, both in the park and apartment houses he designed in Barcelona and in this, his greatest work, the unfinished church of the Holy Family.

It was the attempts—throughout the nineteenth century —to produce a non-historical style that were most fruitful in their influence on the twentieth century, but in the last decade or so before 1900 there were a number of important new departures which also remain influential today. Each was a conscious attempt to find a suitable contemporary style which derived from the architecture itself 'naturally', without relying on any historical precedent. Art Nouveau, to which many of the others were related, was originally, like the historical styles, most obviously characterized by its forms of decoration, but its revolutionary structural characteristics became increasingly important, and it developed into movements which either sought to remove all decoration and present simple forms in the starkest possible way, or aspired consciously to be architecture for the 'Machine Age'.

Art Nouveau (the French called it Modern Style— partly perhaps to distinguish it from the historical styles) was on one side at least the child of the revivals; the Neo-Baroque of the French Second Empire had produced a Neo-Rococo, and the influence of the asymmetric curves and linear surface decoration of Rococo are self-evident in Art Nouveau. But the revolutionary aspects of the style were derived rather from the Arts and Crafts Movement of the second half of the nineteenth century, which had tried to turn away from the impersonal grandeur of the age of industry and commerce and, in terms of furniture and decorations as well as architectural styles, get back to nature (having something in common with today's environmental movements). The 'cottage' style derived from the ideas of Downing, Morris and Webb had been adapted wholeheartedly, not only by Norman Shaw and H. H. Richardson but even by architects such as the prolific Ringstrasse maestro Heinrich Ferstel, who in 1877 helped found the 'Viennese Cottage Association', to build picturesque villas for the respectable middle classes in the new suburbs of Greater Vienna. Elsewhere, architects had grasped the essentials of the development, most notably C. F. Voysey (1857–1941) in England, whose small country houses are models of simplicity, without any of the doctrinaire starkness of later decades, and demonstrate the way the Arts and Crafts had helped towards achieving freer, less rigid architectural forms. But the influence of the decorative arts on Art Nouveau was even more decisive. A fluid linear style with patterns derived from organic forms had been developed in furniture, glass, metalwork and ceramics, and it was the application of this to architecture that had such far-reaching results.

It led to a more sculptural treatment of buildings, and this in turn brought architects' attention back to the conscious manipulation of light and space, and their fully architectural use of cast iron and glass served these ends. Sometimes the cast iron predominates, appearing in characteristic sinuous Art Nouveau curves in great

RIGHT **Hall of Hotel Eetvelde, Brussels;** *V. Horta, 1894–1901.* Around 1900 the most original architecture in Europe was coming from Austria and from Belgium; the Belgian style, of which Horta was the leading practitioner, was the more linear, and made full use of the free forms that can be achieved in wrought iron, often used in conjunction with glass.
BELOW **Sezession Building, Vienna;** *J. Olbrich, 1898–9.* The Viennese Sezession group took advantage of the liberation from historical styles to create a strongly geometrical architecture composed of clearly defined volumes and masses. Here, apart from the gilded wrought-iron dome, the decoration is confined to shallow reliefs, using characteristic motifs, on the wall surfaces.

swirls of banisters and other decorative work on staircases, entrance halls, balconies and façades of houses, or for the famous Metro stations in Paris by Hector Guimard (1867–1942) and in Vienna by Otto Wagner (1841–1918). Sometimes the glass is more important, as in the superb shop-fronts of Brussels, Paris or Berlin, in artists' studios, or in glass roofing. Brussels became one of the chief centres of Art Nouveau architecture and the hall of the Hotel Eetvelde by Victor Horta (1861–1947) shows the combination of iron and glass in a beautifully delicate structure, serving both to give rich illumination and to define the architectural space. This building shows too how the decorative style of Art Nouveau was not just overlaid on a loose structural form (although, of course, many of the untalented architects who simply imitated the decoration did exactly that), but that the interest in simple clearly-defined geometric forms is—apparently contradictarily—equally characteristic.

This is seen much more clearly in the work of the Viennese Sezession group, who in all their work—furniture, metalwork, applied arts and graphic design—tended to convert the free-flowing lines of French and Belgian Art Nouveau into more geometrical formal patterns. Their headquarters, built by Joseph Olbrich (1867–1908), with contributions to the decoration by brother members of the group, including the painter Gustav Klimt (1862–1918), shows the combination of the simplest geometric forms used in a free and unconventional—but strongly articulated—way, with formalized decorations in both metal and stucco based on natural forms. The Sezession group were strongly influenced not only by the Arts and Crafts Movement in Britain, but also particularly strongly by Charles Rennie Mackintosh (1868–1928), the leading exponent of the 'Glasgow style'. Mackintosh was both architect and furniture designer, and it is significant that almost all his furniture was designed for the interiors of his own buildings, to form an integral part of the architecture. His most original interiors—for Miss Cranston's Tea Rooms—have been destroyed (though they have been reconstructed for exhibitions), but the monumental Glasgow School of Art shows his tightly controlled fantasy in the use of asymmetry to enliven the well-proportioned geometric forms.

An entirely different aspect of Art Nouveau is seen in the work of the Spanish architect Antoni Gaudí (1852–1926), whose unfinished church of the Sagrada Familia is perhaps the most extraordinary of many works he built in Barcelona. His buildings often seem to be conceived more as sculpture on a gigantic scale, and his use of cut stone enhances this effect, but at the same time he is exploring new ways of relating masses and space in the same way as the architects of the Sezession or Mackintosh.

Although Art Nouveau had started out as a new decorative style to supersede the historical styles which dominated the nineteenth century—and although for many architects this was as far as it went—the movement contained a more radical element which was working towards an entirely new conception of architecture, in which decoration played only an incidental part, or even was rejected altogether. 'Ornament is crime' said Adolf Loos (1870–1933), a Viennese architect who went beyond the ideas of the Sezessionists to create a severely plain style; yet even this has to be seen as a logical

development from the Art Nouveau movements, as does the work of the German Peter Behrens (1868–1940). He was a leading member of the German *Werkbund*, one of the many associations of artists and craftsmen—the Sezession group was of course another—that was founded in the period around 1900, to give a unity of purpose to men working in different fields of art, architecture and design. In particular, unlike William Morris's Arts and Crafts Movement of the previous century, the *Werkbund* wanted to develop an art for the Machine Age, that accepted modern industrial production. Behrens's work was largely in the industrial field; he was overall design and architectural consultant to the AEG electrical company, and the complex of buildings he designed as their factory and headquarters in Berlin shows his qualities as an architect. The buildings are composed of simple geometric forms, with huge areas of glass windows set in the massive masonry. There are no frills, but the masses are given definition by slight setting forward or setting back of elements, and an extraordinary balance is achieved even on this gigantic scale.

ABOVE **Glasgow School of Art;** *C. R. Mackintosh, 1897–1909.*
Mackintosh's work combines geometric, linear (the iron balconies) and sculptural elements in a composition of studied asymmetry.
BELOW LEFT **Stockholm City Hall;** *Ragnar Östberg, 1909–23.*
Scandinavian architects combined traditional styles and materials with a new simplicity of form.
BELOW RIGHT **AEG Turbine factory, Berlin;** *P. Behrens, 1909.*
The acceptance of the machine by architects finally broke down the old distinction between architects and engineers.

Although there was considerable mobility among the architects of the avant-garde—the Sezessionist Joseph Hoffmann (1870–1956) built a house in Brussels for the banker Stoclet, with superb interior decorations by Klimt; Mackintosh designed for clients in Vienna and Munich; Loos for clients in Paris; the influential Belgian Henri van de Velde (1863–1957), one of the most abstract of the Art Nouveau designers, worked on projects for Paris and for a number of German cities, finally becoming director of the new School of Arts and Crafts at Weimar—their work was not fully accepted, and in the great cities of Europe in the years before the First World War historical styles still predominated, becoming grander and more massive as new methods of construction were adopted. The Ritz Hotel in Piccadilly is the first steel-framed building to have been put up in London, but in its appearance it belongs entirely to the current French Empire Neo-Baroque—not a bad example, only something of an anachronism. Throughout the first half of the twentieth century the historical styles persisted alongside buildings of the developing modern tradition, only gradually being superseded by these and by 'modernistic' architecture, which imitated the externals of modern buildings, without taking account of their fundamental characteristics. The emphasis in this chapter is on the growth of modern architecture, but the background of taste at the time the new buildings were put up should be kept in mind.

The change often came gradually. Sir Edwin Lutyens (1869–1944), for instance, who was responsible for some of the finest small country houses in England in the Norman Shaw–Voysey tradition (often collaborating with the garden designer Gertrude Jekyll), undertook the building of the Viceroy's Palace in New Delhi. This was to be the most imposing building in the whole British Empire, and it foreshadows the even more grandiose—and still shorter-lived—architecture of the Nazi era in Germany. In spite of the scale on which he was working, Lutyens was able to integrate the architectural masses and spaces, using the low dome as a focus for the whole complex. The style is basically in the Classical Renaissance tradition, but using elements derived from Indian architecture—even the plan is based on a Buddhist *stupa*—and keeping the outlines very clean and free from decoration.

ABOVE **House in avenue Rapp, Paris;**
Jules Lavirotte, 1901.
French Art Nouveau followed Belgian styles in its bold sculptural effects and sinuous linear decoration; the most famous examples in Paris are Hector Guimard's Metro stations, but a number of town houses also adopted the modern style. Note the green columns on the top storey.

RIGHT **Church of Steinhof asylum, Vienna;**
O. Wagner, 1903–7.
The colourful decorative scheme and rich materials are used in very simple forms, which echo the geometry of the architecture itself.
Wagner's work and that of contemporary Viennese architects influenced both the International Style and the development of Art Deco architecture.

ABOVE **Palais Stoclet,
Brussels;** *J. Hoffmann,
1905–11.*
The geometric decoration
of the Sezession style is used
here in a way inseparable
from the actual
construction of the house;
the gilt edging friezes either
define the cubic volumes
of the house, or serve to
emphasize those elements,
the windows in particular,
which counter this
geometrical simplicity and
give such a lively interest
to the architecture.
LEFT **Viceroy's Palace,
New Delhi;** *E. Lutyens,
1920–31.*
The planning of New Delhi
by Lutyens and H. Baker is
the last great example of
British imperialist
architecture. Lutyens's
Viceroy's Palace, though
basically revivalist, shows
affinities with the
modern movement in its
simple geometric volumes.

The most revolutionary innovation of the early twentieth century was the development of reinforced concrete, strengthened by steel bars set into it, so that it combined the stress-bearing qualities and malleability of steel with the uncrushability of concrete. Reinforced concrete became the most versatile of all the architect's materials and enormously enlarged the repertory of forms available. Its architectural potentialities were first realized in France by architects who included the visionary planner Tony Garnier (1869–1948); Auguste Perret (1874–1954), who used it for apartment blocks, industrial buildings and a fine church at Le Raincy, near Paris; and Eugène Freyssinet (1879–1962), whose aeroplane hangars at Orly (now destroyed) were each made up of one huge parabolic vault large enough to contain within it the cathedrals of Paris, Chartres and Rheims.

Nevertheless it was not so much the constructional techniques that revolutionized architecture, but revolutionary architecture which adopted and developed the techniques. Immediately following the First World War the pioneers of modern architecture came into their own. Henri van de Velde's successor as director of the Weimar Art School was Walter Gropius (1883–1969), a pupil of Peter Behrens, and in 1925 the school was moved to Dessau as a university of design—the Bauhaus. Owing both its existence and many of its ideals largely to the pre-war associations of artists, the Bauhaus was of incalculable influence in twentieth-century architecture and design. It provided the complete antithesis to the theory that underlay historicism in architecture—that the 'style' should correspond to the representative function of a building or object—insisting that it should be designed (no talk here of 'styling') with the utmost simplicity and solely with its practical function in mind. This was not to deny the aesthetic element in architecture, but rather to say that the most functional is the most beautiful. The buildings of the Bauhaus itself were designed by Gropius, as was an 'estate' of small houses within the city. The Bauhaus (now in sad disrepair) was of extreme simplicity, with one wall entirely filled with glass, a building strangely unimpressive now, with the familiarity of how many millions of square feet of glass and rows of boxlike buildings, but utterly revolutionary in its time. As with the change from Gothic to Renaissance, the transition itself to the new modern aesthetic was gradual, with many glances backward as well as forward, but once established it could be seen to have made a complete break with tradition, of a sort that had not taken place in European art since the Renaissance.

RIGHT **Town Hall, Hilversum;**
W. M. Dudok, 1928–30.
Dudok made bold use of brickwork in wide plain surfaces, relying on windows to vary the texture.

OPPOSITE **Church at Le Raincy, near Paris;**
A. Perret, 1922–3.
Perret's church effectively exploits the characteristics of reinforced concrete in the curving roof and the pierced walls, inset with coloured glass.

The twenties and thirties saw the style developed by many architects, and it became known as the 'International Style' after the 1932 exhibition at the New York Museum of Modert Art, which showed the work of Mies van der Rohe, Le Corbusier, Gropius, J. J. P. Oud, Frank Lloyd Wright and others. At the Bauhaus itself Gropius's two most important followers were Marcel Breuer (b. 1902) and Mies van der Rohe (1886–1969), the latter succeeding Gropius as director of the Bauhaus in 1930. The characteristic simplicity of Mies's style was shown in the German pavilion for the Barcelona exhibition of 1929, but his most significant work was carried out in the USA, where like Gropius and Breuer he emigrated in the years following the Nazis' closure of the Bauhaus. In Holland van de Velde started

RIGHT **Schröder house, Utrecht;** *G. Rietveld, 1924.*
Rietveld's buildings offer a close parallel to the paintings of his companion in the *de Stijl* group, Piet Mondrian; the Schröder house is composed of squares and rectangles in three dimensions, with sparing use of strong primary colours. The abstract nature of the composition is typified by the large slab of the front balcony, which serves to join the upper and lower floors and contradict the known divisions between them.

OPPOSITE **Model of the Bauhaus, Dessau;**
W. Gropius, 1925–6.
The three blocks, serving as, respectively, workshops, student hostel and administrative buildings, are laid out on an asymmetrical plan. The workshop has a curtain wall (bearing none of the load of the building) entirely of glass, through which the steel-frame construction of the building can be seen undisguised. The building is now sadly disfigured.

RIGHT **House in rue Mallet-Stevens, Paris;**
R. Mallet-Stevens, 1926–8.
The influence of Joseph Hoffmann and of the Cubists can be seen in the work of Mallet-Stevens, which represents the Art Deco style in architecture.

OPPOSITE **House of the Soviet, Gorky (Nijni Novgorod);**
A. S. Grinberg, 1929–31.
In the early revolutionary years Russian architects, notably the Constructivists, shared leadership of the modern movement in architecture with the Dutch *de Stijl* group and the Italian Futurists. This work of Grinberg shows bold use of a semi-circular wall in a building of very clean lines.

work soon after the War on his most important commission, the Kröller-Müller Museum in Otterloo, though it was twenty-five years in the building, and the *de Stijl* movement, best known for the work of the painter Piet Mondrian, influenced several notable Dutch architects, J. J. P. Oud (1890–1963), W. M. Dudok (b. 1884), who was architect to the town of Hilversum, and Gerrit Rietveld (1888–1964). Rietveld's Schröder house in Utrecht shows the typical use of contrasting verticals and horizontals, not as simple blocks (as in Dudok's later Hilversum Town Hall), but in a much more complicated play of flat planes with thin profiles, supporting pillars and metal balconies, to produce an abstract construction that is the equivalent of a large-scale sculpture. The same manipulation of geometrical elements into a coherent construction was characteristic of the short-lived Constructivist movement in revolutionary Russia, and of the work of Robert Mallet-Stevens (1886–1945) in Paris, which shows more clearly his indebtedness to the Viennese architects Hoffmann and Loos.

RIGHT **Einstein Observatory, Potsdam;** *E. Mendelsohn, 1919–21.* With its free forms resembling an ocean liner, the observatory was intended to be built in reinforced concrete, but the problems of forming it were too great, and it was largely constructed of brick, coated with cement to look like concrete. This work, together with Hans Poelzig's Great Theatre (1919), with its stalactite ceiling, made Berlin the centre for Expressionism in architecture—a movement which ran both counter and parallel to the course of functional architecture.

BELOW **Falling Water house, Bear Run, Pa.;** *F. L. Wright, 1936.* This, Wright's most famous house, exemplifies his belief that a building should belong to the landscape, so that 'the exterior space will become a natural part of the space within the building.'

A different direction was taken by Erich Mendelsohn, (1887–1953), whose work can be seen as the most representative architecture of the Expressionist movement: dramatic, highly charged, making use of sweeping curves and strong contrasts, with its roots in the more sculptural architecture of the turn of the century.

This more romantic approach was also favoured in Scandinavia, where modern architecture was readily accepted and which was to become one of the most fruitful centres of modern design. The most original architect was the Finn Alvar Aalto (b. 1898), whose public library at Viipuri (now in the USSR) has an undulating timber roof, so constructed for acoustic reasons to deaden sound, but also an aesthetic innovation of great influence.

Aalto's library is typical of the period in another respect, that it was a municipal commission. This was the pioneer age of effective socialism, and public authorities and architects alike believed in the potentiality of the new architecture to cause a revolution in social conditions. Slums were cleared and huge apartment blocks were built for workers, with every attempt made to provide not only a decent and well-built place to live, but also a good urban environment, with gardens, libraries, shops and other facilities. It was the equivalent of the garden city for the middle classes pioneered in the last quarter of the nineteenth century. Increasingly, in Europe and revolutionary Russia, the need was seen for co-ordinated urban planning, to replace the mixture of

slums and speculative building that had everywhere been the original accompaniment to the industrial revolution and the growth of urban populations. Authorities in the Scandinavian countries and in Holland were among the leaders, and so too, in spite of the enormous problems they had to overcome in the social and economic consequences of the War, was the socialist municipality of Vienna, though far the most forward-looking and ultimately influential of all the planner-architects was Charles-Edouard Jeanneret, known as Le Corbusier (1887–1965). The acceptance of the basic principles of the Bauhaus meant that there was an incalculable difference between these projects and the demoralizing 'charitable dwellings' erected by nineteenth-century philanthropists. The attempt was now made to create an urban environment, allowing for the use of private motor-cars and taking account of public transport facilities, that would be good for people to live in. Even the most well-intentioned schemes have not, with use, always proved successful—the particularly acute social problems of the mid-twentieth century and the dominating role of the motor-car were not fully anticipated—but a comparison of any of these schemes with the hideous wastelands that fringe urban centres in the USA, where authorities were much more resistant to planning, shows how much was nevertheless achieved.

The overwhelming achievement of the USA was in work undertaken for rich patrons, whether private or public. Until the arrival of the Bauhaus architects expelled from Germany, the dominant progressive influence had been Frank Lloyd Wright (1869–1959), a pupil of Louis Sullivan, who, quite independent of European influences, had been developing a native architectural style for the modern world. Wright's career spans the whole first half of the twentieth century, and from the earliest years, before 1914, he was working mainly on private houses and he had already shown his concern to design houses 'from the inside', from the living spaces, and also for making the architecture a part of the surrounding landscape. He made use of the latest technology, including construction with reinforced concrete, but one of his main sources of inspiration was the traditional architecture of Japan. He also completed in 1922 the Imperial Hotel in Tokyo and his work forms an important link between east and west in the formation of the truly international style which has dominated world architecture since the mid-century. One of his boldest projects was the house Falling Water at Bear Run, Penn., with its use of concrete and rough stonework in a dramatic landscape setting.

But Wright's influence was for a long time very limited. The majority of monumental buildings in the United States of the inter-war years—and later—still owed allegiance to the historical styles of the nineteenth century. These were incorporated in the new skyscrapers in an extraordinary way, usually affecting only the main entrance and the top floors of the building, where one might sprout a wealth of Gothic pinnacles, while another supported a French Baroque château. The design for the new Tribune Tower in Chicago was open to competition and attracted an extraordinary variety of entries, from the anthropomorphic (the top floors as the head of an Indian chief) to the avant-garde, including projects from Adolf Loos, from the Bauhaus architects and a design by the Finn Eliel Saarinen (1873–1950), which if built would have been a worthy successor to the Chicago architecture of the previous century. But the design chosen was modelled on the flamboyant Gothic Tour de Beurre at Rouen, an anachronistic monument to lost opportunity.

It might have been thought that the nineteenth century had exhausted all usable historical styles, but a new

one emerged as characteristic of the 1920s and 1930s. Undoubtedly the use of plain geometric shapes and flat planes that characterized much of the new architecture around 1900, and the industrial architecture in particular, had an affinity with and may in some cases have been influenced by the monumental architecture of Crete and Mycenae, of Egypt and of Latin America uncovered by archeologists. In trying to create a new massively monumental architecture suited to the Machine Age, architects began to borrow extensively from these sources and from the Sezession and other geometrical Art Nouveau styles, and the Moderne and Art Deco styles were the result. The Richfield Building in Los Angeles (now destroyed) and the Chrysler Building in New York were two fine buildings in this style, relying heavily on richness of materials and decoration, but adapting from the sources in a highly original way. On another level this was adopted as the architectural style of the Jazz Age and the heyday of Hollywood, and in a wide variety of forms appeared in cinemas, music-halls, shops, hotels, restaurants and ocean liners. With their emphasis on surface decoration both inside and out, the architects of the Art Deco movement were in complete opposition to the ideals of the Bauhaus, and certainly their interiors can be oppressive, in contrast with the light, open simplicity of Bauhaus architecture; but there is a liveliness about their decoration that often contrasts favourably with the stark, dull exterior of many derivative modern buildings.

ABOVE **Tribune Tower, Chicago;** *Raymond Hood and John Mead Howells, 1922–5.*
This is the notorious example of 'skyscraper Gothic', based on the Tour de Beurre at Rouen, that was chosen in competition against projects by Eliel Saarinen, Adolf Loos, Gropius and Breuer, and many others. Hood's later work shifted easily into plainer styles and included the old McGraw-Hill Tower in New York (1932), startlingly covered with green tiles, and a share in the design of the massive Rockefeller Center there.

LEFT **Apex of Chrysler Building, New York;** *William Van Alen, 1929.*
The first skyscraper to top 1000 feet, the Chrysler Building is one of the finest surviving examples of the American Moderne style (the more machine-orientated side of Art Deco), with much geometric patterning—the sunburst was a favourite motif—streamlining and formalized sculpture. Materials of interior and exterior alike were extravagant, and Van Alen made pioneering use of aluminium and stainless steel in architecture. The great skyscrapers were built as expressions of industrial or commercial power, and no style was more effective or more fitting than the Moderne.

The craving for monumentality became even more acute in the public architecture of the totalitarian régimes of the thirties. The architects of Mussolini's Italy turned for their inspiration to the architecture of ancient Rome, and this affinity seems to have led to some genuinely impressive buildings. The Railway Station in Milan has all the paraphernalia of Fascist symbolism, but approaches the same imposing, if rather empty, grandeur of the late monuments of ancient Rome. However, in Russia, buildings like the Lomonosov State University, massive and entirely uninteresting, seem to epitomize the complete lack of humanity of the Stalinist régime and the suppression of so many of the truly progressive forces of the early years of the revolution, while the work of Hitler's architect Albert Speer combines mediocrity and absurd *folie de grandeur* in its use of a 'purified' Neo-Grecian style on a giant, megalomaniac scale. The sterility of his work is in depressing contrast to the imagination and vision of the architects of the Bauhaus, who until 1933 had led the way for their colleagues throughout the world.

After they had left Germany, Gropius, Breuer and Mendelsohn all worked for a time in England and exerted a profound influence on contemporary English architects. The work of Maxwell Fry (b. 1899) in particular, who was for a time in partnership with Gropius, shows strong Bauhaus influence, both in its simple forms and its deep social commitment.

After the Second World War the International Style dominated the scene. Reconstruction all over Europe gave architects opportunities to work on projects on a

OPPOSITE **Railway Station, Milan;** *Ulisse Stacchini, c. 1910–31.*
Although most of the work was done in the twenties, the station is a curious mixture of Liberty (Italian Art Nouveau) and Fascist styles. More typical of the dictatorships in Italy and Germany was a massive Neo-Grecian style, sometimes shorn of all ornament, so that the columns appear as stark rectangular posts.

RIGHT **Impington Village College, Cambs.;** *W. Gropius and Maxwell Fry, 1936–40.*
Here the humanist principles of the Bauhaus are put into action; the classrooms are at ground level with walls all of windows, so that the building gives shelter, but forms no barrier between the children and the natural environment.

ABOVE **Tuberculosis Sanatorium, Paimio, Finland;** *A. Aalto, 1929–33.*
The sanatorium is designed to give first consideration to the needs of the patients; each has a private room in the block illustrated, with a large south-facing window.

OPPOSITE **Lomonosov University, Moscow;** *Lev Rudnev, 1949–53.*
Dehumanized Neo-Classicism on a huge scale was typical of Russia in the Stalin era.

RIGHT **Lobby of Radio City Music Hall, New York;** *1932.*
A huge theatre and cinema complex within the Rockefeller Center, Radio City is outstanding for its Art Deco interior decoration, carried out under the supervision of Donald Deskey. Every element, from the 29-foot chromium and glass chandeliers to the furniture, the murals and the carpets, is a part of the grand design.

very extensive scale, and Le Corbusier for one was able to realize some of his most radical and ambitious schemes, including the planning of a new capital city for Punjab at Chandigarh, and the execution of several 'Unités d'Habitation'. Although he had carried out some important public commissions in the twenties and thirties, Le Corbusier's most far-reaching projects belong to the years after 1945. As early as 1922 he had proposed plans for a city of three million inhabitants with high-rise tower blocks and wide tracts of green parkland; he developed a new system of proportions based on the human body, the Modulor; and he applied this to the standardization of constructional elements in the buildings; he made use of reinforced concrete structures which allowed large parts of the buildings to be supported on struts, giving far greater space at ground level; and many of his buildings are made up of standardized prefabricated elements. The project which embodied his ideas in their most concentrated form was the Unité d'Habitation, with living and social facilities for two thousand people (four hundred apartments) concentrated in one tower block surrounded by parks: 'a revolutionary event, sun, space and greenery. If you want to raise a family in privacy, in silence and in natural surroundings . . .' The first Unité to be built was in Marseilles in 1947–52 and a number of others followed, embodying changes as a result of criticisms of certain elements of the original Unité.

In contrast to the Unités were the luxury apartment blocks built by Mies van der Rohe around Lake Michigan in Chicago. Mies was the most prolific of the Bauhaus architects in America and his buildings are of extreme simplicity, making their effect by their size and by the combinations of polished surfaces—plain or tinted glass, marble, bronze, aluminium, steel—the reinforced concrete frame often being disguised by a curtain wall of metal and glass. In the Seagram Building, designed by Mies in collaboration with the American architect Philip Johnson (b. 1906), not only are the most luxurious materials employed, but the building is set back ninety feet from the street with an open plaza in front, to detach it from the adjoining buildings. Mies van der Rohe's late works are a peak of the International Style, achieving a purity which has made it necessary for architects of originality to attempt new departures. In spite of its internationalism, the modern movement con-

LEFT **Unité d'Habitation (Cité Radieuse), Marseilles;** *Le Corbusier, 1947–52.*
The Unité is a complete 'village' with shops, libraries, etc., reached from interior streets, and a huge recreation area on the roof. The use of bare concrete is enlivened by the strong primary colours of the window surrounds.

BELOW LEFT **Commonwealth Promenade Apartments, Chicago;** *Mies van der Rohe, 1953–6.*
The high-rise buildings of Mies show the use of the steel frame and curtain wall of glass in the purest possible way. The unadorned repetition is made acceptable partly by the large scale (small-scale imitations do not create the same effect) and partly by the use of reflective glass and metals (here aluminium) that give a rich overall surface texture. The use of the curtain wall logically separates the two functions of a wall, load bearing (the skeleton) and environmental control (the skin).

BELOW **Guggenheim Museum, New York;** *F. L. Wright, 1943–59.*
The unflagging originality of Frank Lloyd Wright (he started work in Adler and Sullivan's office in the 1880s) is unparalleled in architectural history. The exterior of the Guggenheim reflects the interior ramp, around which the works of art are displayed, in an expressive form, but it remains unrelated to the surrounding buildings.

LEFT **Seagram Building, New York;** *Mies van der Rohe and P. Johnson, completed 1958.*
The curtain wall of a tower-block acts as a protective screen, but makes no dictates about internal arrangement, so that the building, or different parts of it, can be adapted to a wide variety of uses. Although Mies has been criticized for his all-purpose buildings, this is one of their most fundamental qualities.

BELOW **Art and Architecture Faculty, Yale;** *P. Rudolph, 1961–3.*
The raw concrete surfaces of Brutalist architecture are not easy to handle successfully, although it has become one of the most widely adopted modern styles. Rudolph's buildings refer back to the intricate linear compositions of *de Stijl* and to the more massive work of F. L. Wright, using the wide expanses of window to relieve the harshness of the concrete surfaces.

BOTTOM **Plaza of the Three Powers, Brasilia;** *L. Costa and O. Niemeyer, 1956–60.*
The architects adopted a strongly sculptural approach, consciously in the tradition of Gaudí, though employing geometrical forms, with constrasted verticals and horizontals, straight lines and curves. Their work was influenced by the more Expressionist side of Le Corbusier, as well as by his ideas on city planning.

tains many strands of development, which have led to an increasing variety of building styles.

Frank Lloyd Wright continued working after the War and his Guggenheim Museum in New York impresses visitors with its striking originality, although it owes more to Mendelsohn and the Expressionist movement than to more recent developments, and is much less successful for displaying works of art than, say, the new Lateran Museum in the Vatican Palace, designed by the engineer-architect Pier Luigi Nervi (b. 1891). More typical of Nervi's work are his sportsdromes in Rome, which are designed deliberately to show off feats of constructional virtuosity.

One of the largest of all new commissions was that of the Brazilian government for a new capital city, Brasilia. This work has been under the control of Lucio Costa (b. 1902), though the most important buildings are the work of Oscar Niemeyer (b. 1907), a Brazilian pupil of Le Corbusier, who worked together with his master on a number of important municipal projects in Rio de Janeiro in the 1930s. Niemeyer, while keeping to Le Corbusier's principles, has favoured a more picturesque style, contrasting simple slab-like buildings with others that exploit to the full the sculptural qualities of concrete.

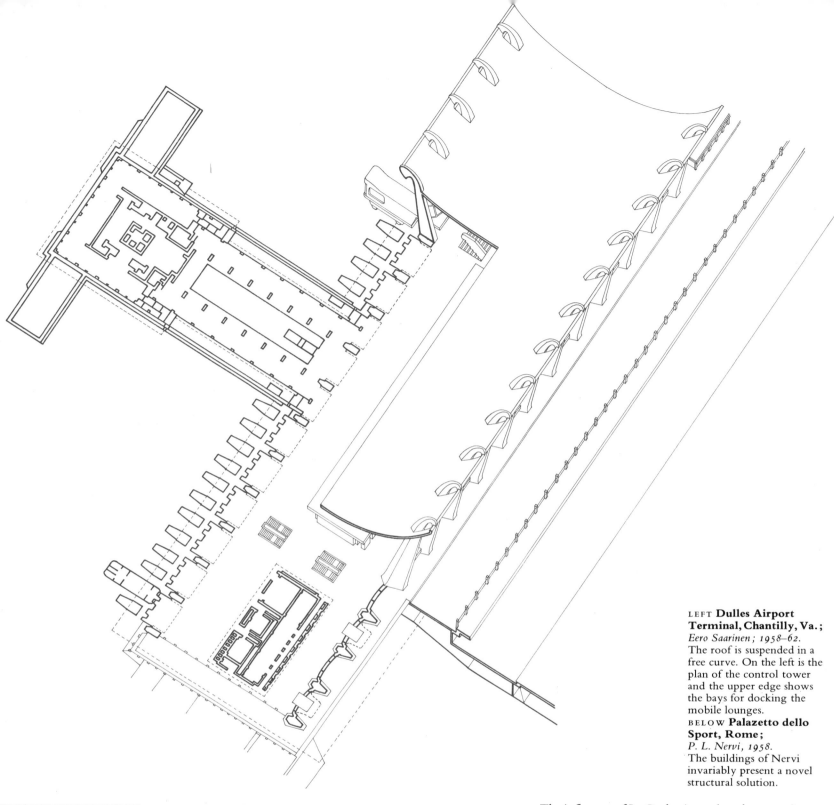

The influence of Le Corbusier and, at the same time, a greater appreciation of the more expressionist elements in the International movement characterized much of the architecture of the fifties and sixties. Forms were freer, but nevertheless practical functions—designing from the inside out—were put first. The Dulles International Air Terminal by Eero Saarinen (1910–61) is a superb example of this. Practical considerations of passenger mobility—adopting a highly original solution—were the prime factors considered by the architect, who not only makes use of a beautifully engineered structure, but seems also to take delight in showing exactly how it is done and relishes the expressive curves of the roof, which is suspended from dramatically outward-leaning concrete supports.

The same enjoyment of forms dictated by practical necessities, though not on such an outstanding level of achievement, is seen in the Philharmonie concert hall in Berlin by Hans Scharoun (b. 1893). The tentlike roof

was dictated in part at least by acoustical considerations,
since convexity diffuses sounds, but the description of
the hall by the architect himself (who had been active in
the Expressionist movement before the War) is significant. He sees it in terms of landscape design, a valley
with the orchestra in its hollow, and the rows of seats as
vineyards rising on each side, while the roof is a skyscape.
Equally expressive is the work of the outstanding Japanese architect, Kenzo Tange (b. 1913). Trained in the
traditions of Frank Lloyd Wright and Le Corbusier, he
has both designed buildings which make use of heavy
concrete members and made radical departures in constructional techniques, particularly in the roof suspen-
sion of his superb Olympic Gymnasium.

The more rigidly geometric abstract constructions of
de Stijl have been taken up again by architects such as
Paul Rudolph (b. 1918), whose building for the Art
and Architecture Faculty at Yale contrasts massive
rough-surfaced concrete with fragile windows, giving
strong vertical-horizontal contrasts. The emphasis both
on the mass of the material and its undisguised surface
have led this style to be labelled Brutalism. It has found
an international reception, and many English architects
in particular have seemed almost obsessed with the
aggressive display of the naked constructional materials
both on exteriors and interiors—though Scandinavian
influence has sometimes led to a choice of more com-
fortable materials than concrete (which the streaking
quickly caused by English climate and pollution make
a particularly ugly material for exteriors), the use of a
wide variety of woods often providing one of the most
attractive features.

FAR LEFT AND LEFT **John Hancock Tower, Chicago;** *Skidmore, Owings and Merrill, 1969–70.* **Lake Point Tower, Chicago;** *G. Schipporeit and J. Heinrich, 1968.* Both buildings exemplify the liberation of form created by new engineering techniques; Lake Point Tower, by pupils of Mies van der Rohe, adapts his structures to a clover-leaf plan, and is impressive both for its sheer virtuosity and because of its commanding position on Lake Michigan; but the John Hancock Tower, with offices, 705 apartments, health club, 'the world's fastest automatic elevators' and its 'gourmet restaurant with a view of four states' beneath the 'Crown of Lights', is a sad monument to consumer society.

BELOW **Opera House, Sydney;** *Jørn Utzon, 1959–73.* Utzon's romantic design is a return to the sculpture in architecture of Gaudí; its construction has been fraught with controversy and Utzon's plans have been altered, though the exterior form reflects his original designs.

The extraordinary flexibility of new materials has posed as much of a problem for architects as it has in some ways eased their task. The severity of the International Style provided a real alternative to the stylistic searchings of the preceding century, but where to go from there? There is more work than ever for architects to undertake, and on a far greater scale, yet there are so many more considerations to be borne in mind. They have to design not only public buildings which provide good working conditions, but also satisfactory living areas and a good urban environment—taking into consideration the problems posed by the motor-car and the provision of transport facilities, and facing up to the restrictions and requirements of developers, planners, sociologists and politicians as well as the welcome, but often inconvenient, agitation of the conservationist lobby. It is inevitable that failures are more numerous, more obviously offensive and destructive to the environment, and more inconvenient and socially destructive to many more people. Attempts to improve on the Miesian simplicity by making it less simple, or, worse still, to try and seduce conservative public opinion by combining the International Style with traditional architectural forms, have now disfigured cities throughout the world.

Mies van der Rohe's influence has been felt most directly by architects such as Philip Johnson, whose work has a tendency to be stylized and academic, and the partnerships Skidmore, Owings and Merrill, and Schipporeit and Heinrich, who have adopted Mies's

materials and constructional methods, while adopting more mannered forms. The John Hancock Tower in Chicago is too close for comfort to the tradition of megalomaniac architecture which has been only too persistent for the past two hundred years. By contrast, the new Opera House in Sydney, nearing completion as this is written, takes full advantage of constructional techniques and is architecture at its most extravagantly picturesque. Quite different again is the increasing use of prefabricated units of prestressed concrete, a technique pioneered by Marcel Breuer and Le Corbusier requiring—and seldom receiving—an extreme sensitivity of handling to avoid monotony.

The options for the future seem to be open. Will we see prefabrication taken to its logical conclusion, as in the complete living units designed to be fitted into one another in a variety of ways, shown in the Habitat apartments exhibited in Montreal in 1967 and now in use there? A covered urban environment, built in science fiction style, like the Munich Olympic complex? Floating cities, as designed by Tange and others, as a solution to urban overcrowding? An extension of the geodesic domes of Richard Buckminster Fuller (b. 1895), which have been constructed on his space-frame principle in all sizes and from a wide variety of materials? Plug-in cities in Pop style, as projected by the British Archigram group? Or the ecological house, which uses solar energy and recycling techniques to be entirely independent of any external power or food supplies?

Acknowledgments

The author and publishers wish to thank the following for their kind permission to reproduce the photographs in this book:
Marianne Adelmann, 62 top, 66 top, 69 top, 109; (Weidenfeld) 69 below
AF Photographic Library, 11 below left, 124 below
Architectural Review (Dell and Wainwright), 119 top
David Attenborough (Weidenfeld), 20 top
Austrian National Tourist Office (Hans Huber), 104 below
Robert Belton, 121 top right
Tim Benton (Weidenfeld), 74 top
Burckhardt Verlag, 113 top, 115 centre, 119 below left
Camera Press (Fritz Prenzel), 72 top
Canada House, 102 below
J. Allan Cash, 92 top, 98 below right, 111 below left
Cement and Concrete Association, 114 top
Courtauld Institute of Art, 98 below left, 102 top right, 114 centre and below, 115 top; (Weidenfeld), 33 below, 40 below right [National Monuments Record—Crown copyright]
Bruce Cunningham-Werdnigg, 99 below, 121 below right
D. K. Dowley, 97 below left
Elsevier Sequoia S.A., 64 centre
Werner Forman, 11 below right, 17 top, 18 below, 19 right, 20 below, 21 top, 26 both, 31, 39 top right, 45 below, 47, 49 top left and below right, 50 below right, 50–1, 52 below, 55 below, 88 top right and below right, 91 below right, 92 centre and bottom; (Weidenfeld), 24 top, 71 below, 110 below
Giraudon, 96 top
Sonia Halliday, 10 below, 23, 24 below right, 25 below, 38 left, 52 top; (F. H. C. Birch), 53 right
Stephen Harrison, 12 all, 21 below, 24 below left, 37 left, 45 top left, 63 below; 75 below left, 76 top, 84 top
Hirmer Verlag, 16 top, 17 below, 28 below left, 50 top
Michael Holford, 10 below, 15, 19 left, 43, 44 top, 49 top right, 61 below, 70 top, 80 below left, 97 below right; (Ann Mowlem), 18 top
Angelo Hornak, 38 right, 57, 58 top right, 59, 68 top, 80 top and below right, 97 centre left, 99 centre, 100 both, 105 top, 107 both, 117 both, 120 below left and right, 121 left, 124 top left and right
Humboldt University, Berlin, 116 top
Italian State Tourist Office, 122 below
Japan Information Centre, 123 top right
A. F. Kersting, 25 top, 27 below, 32, 33 right, 35 centre, 36 top left, 37 top, 40 below left, 44 below, 54 top right, 59 below, 63 centre, 65, 70 below, 71, 73 both, 75 below right, 78 top left and top right, 79 both, 81 top, 85 below left, 95, 96 below, 98 top, 101 top, 104 top, 106 top
Landesbildstelle, Berlin, 111 below right
Emily Lane, 61 top right
Mansell Collection (Alinari), 118 top
Bildarchiv Foto Marburg, 28 top right, 110 top; (Weidenfeld), 36 below left, 45 top right
Mas, Barcelona, 34 top; (Weidenfeld), 75 top
Muzeul de Istoria, Rumania, 39 top left
Novosti Press Agency, 118 below
A. Ohmayer, 77 top left
Ontario House, 123 top left
B. Orr, Carlisle, Mass., 106 below
Picturepoint, 125 all
George Rainbird (Werner Neumeister), 105 below
Jean Roubier (Weidenfeld), 40 top
M. Sakamoto (Weidenfeld), 88 left
Scala, 2–3,7, 27 top left, 33 top left, 34 below, 35 top, 42 left top and below, 58 below right, 60, 68 below, 72 below, 76 below, 84 below, 86 below
Cosmo Sileo, 119 below right
Staatsbibliothek, Berlin, 99 top; (Siegfried Lauterwasser), 123 below
Stoedtner-Klemm, 115 below
Studio Seven, 110–1
Leonard von Matt (Weidenfeld), 66 below
Weidenfeld and Nicolson (Eric Berry), 13 top; (Kerry Dundas), 50 below left, 64 top, 77 below; (Ian Graham), 49 below left, 53 left, 54 top left and below, 55 top, 61 top left, 63 top, 64 below, 81 below, 83, 85 top and below right, 86 top, 87 both, 90, 91 top and below left, 92–3, 97 top; (John Marmaras), 102 left; (Edwin Smith), 13 below, 58 left, 74 below, 77 top right, 78 left
Western Pennsylvania Conservancy, Pittsburgh, 116 below
Jeremy Whitaker, 27 top right, 62 below
Roger Wood, 28 top left
Yan (Weidenfeld), 36 right
ZEFA (Stuller) 112 below
Joseph Ziolo, 16 below; (Faillet), 112 top; (René Percheron), 39 below; (Promophot), 11 top; (René Roland), 113 below; (Phédon Salou), 42 right, 101 below, 120 top; (J. Verroust), 35 below

The drawings on the endpapers and on pages 1, 8–9, 29, 41, 48, 67, 89, 103 and 122 were prepared specially for this book by Enzo di Grazia. The author wishes particularly to thank him for his help, and also Mrs Myra Clarke, John Curtis of Weidenfeld and Nicolson, Werner Forman, Angelo Hornak, Trevor Vincent and Jeremy Whitaker for their help and advice.

Jacket illustrations: (front and back), S. Maria della Salute, Venice (Angelo Hornak); (front flap), Lake Point Tower, Chicago (Angelo Hornak); (back flap), Temple of the Emerald Buddha, Bangkok (Van Phillips)

Index

References to works illustrated and their architects are in **bold** type, to the text in roman type, and to the captions in *italics*.

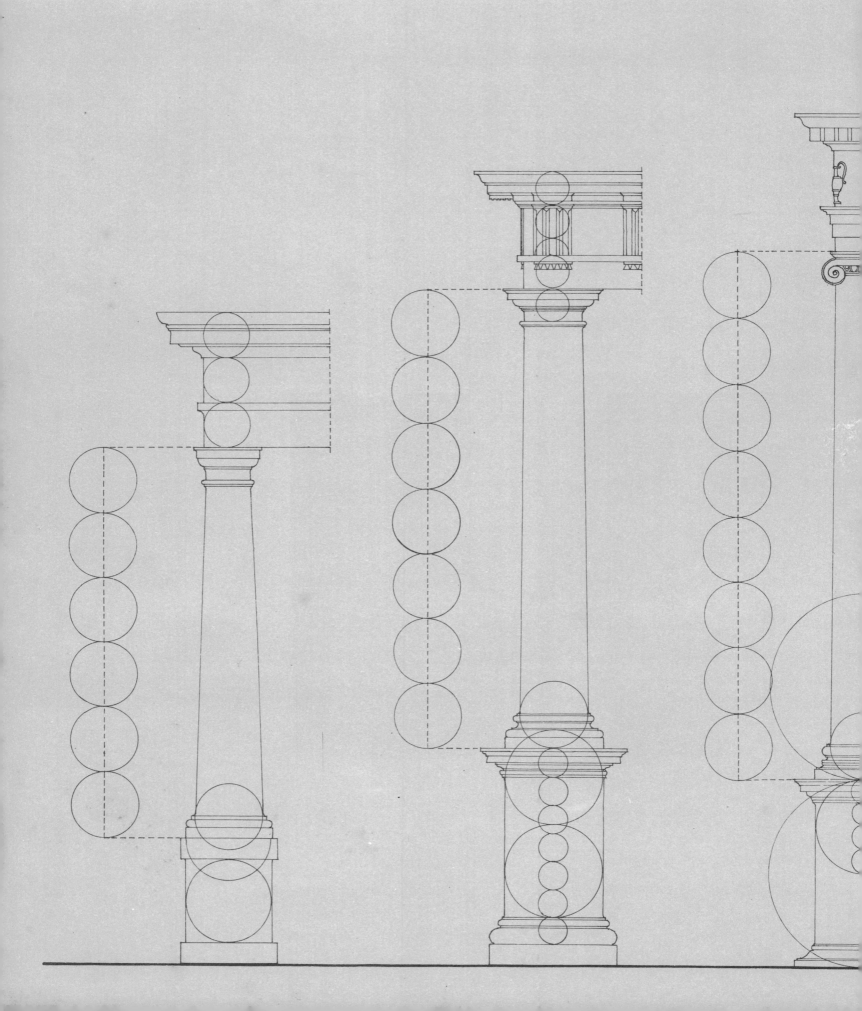